TH

Yishai Shiloh

Production by eBookPro Publishing
www.ebook-pro.com

THE MEDITATING MIND
Yishai Shiloh

Copyright © 2024 Yishai Shiloh

All rights reserved; no parts of this book may be reproduced
or transmitted in any form or by any means, electronic
or mechanical, including photocopying, recording, taping,
or by any information retrieval system, without
the permission, in writing, of the author.

Translation from Hebrew: Dr. Jonathan Boxman
Editing: Matthew Berman

Contact: yishaishiloh@gmail.com

ISBN 9798339319771

THE MEDITATING MIND

*A simple meditation guide to declutter your mind,
elevate your mental health,
and find inner peace in a stress-free life*

YISHAI SHILOH

Contents

META-COGNITION
Thoughts about Thoughts 23

MEDITATION — GUIDANCE
Special cases 26

META-COGNITION
The cause, the record and what lies between 29

MEDITATION — GUIDANCE
Pre-Exercise 1 Questionnaire 36
Exercise 1 39

META-COGNITION
Physical evidence 48
Post-Exercise 1 Report 59

META-COGNITION
Seeing what is missing 60

MEDITATION — GUIDANCE
Meditation tools 67

META-COGNITION
The Exception Requiring Explanation 78

MEDITATION – GUIDANCE
Exercise 2 82
Post-Exercise 2 Report 95

META-COGNITION
Seeing is believing 96

MEDITATION — GUIDANCE
Exercise 3 98
Post-Exercise 3 Report..100

META-COGNITION
What is a presumption? 101

MEDITATION — GUIDANCE
Exercise 4 110
Post-Exercise 4 Report..120

META-COGNITION
There is No confusion in heaven 121

MEDITATION — GUIDANCE
Exercise 5 125
Post-Exercise 5 Report.. 133

META-COGNITION
Knowledge and internalization.. 134

MEDITATION — GUIDANCE
Exercise 6 136
Post-Exercise 6 Report.. 139

SUMMARY
Meditation is the drug of life 140

TO CONCLUDE
In conclusion 145

APPENDIX A
The essence of matter 147

APPENDIX B
The basis of all religions... 154

APPENDIX C
Separation of law from justice in religious legal systems 160

What is meditation?

Before we begin explaining how to practice meditation let us start by asking: Why is practicing meditation necessary? What is the use in it?

The short answer is that meditation is a simple mental technique, which brings the meditator into a unique state of serenity, wakefulness and fulfillment. Meditation, when correctly practiced, relieves stress, increases intelligence and problem-solving skills, and it improves the practitioner's general feeling and quality of life. These are the basic reasons why meditation should be practiced.

What is the definition of meditation? It is hard to answer this question unambiguously, though we shall make an attempt to do so in this manual. There are countless mental exercises defined as "meditation" exercises that seemingly have nothing in common. What, nonetheless, is the common denominator? We shall try to answer this question later.

There are also many mental exercises that have been described as "meditative" though in actuality they involve self-hypnosis, not meditation.

The difficulty in defining what meditation is, and explaining how it works, have lead some meditation courses and instructors to focus exclusively on the practical outcome and enjoy the results, rather than occupying themselves with the question of how it all works.

I believe that the theoretical aspect of meditation is also important, and this manual will not neglect it. Of course, all that is written in this manual is the fruit of my own personal research and relies on my own experience, which I have decided to share with you, the readers.

Throughout this manual I occasionally repeat myself in order to emphasize an important issue, or in order to present it from a different angle, or narrow in on specific aspects of it, or to add things that were not mentioned before. You may be tempted to skip over material which strikes you as being familiar, but it is important your read it all attentively, for this will help you understand the practice.

So what is meditation, actually?

In my opinion, meditation can be summed up, in a single sentence: It is the release of consciousness from the bonds imposed on it by the body. When consciousness is set free, it naturally returns to its primordial state of purity, serenity, and joy, as it was before life's day-to-day anxieties drove it to frenzied agitation.

The return of consciousness to its roots is a process that takes place on its own. Our own role is merely to release consciousness from these bonds, and we do that through meditation.

But what precisely are the earthly bonds we seek to sever that are chaining the consciousness to the body?

The body provides consciousness with stimuli of pleasure and pain through the nervous system, and it is they who bind and enslave consciousness to the needs of the body, forcing man to pursue pleasure and flee pain, leaving him constantly restless.

In meditation we seek to release ourselves, if only a little bit, from the hold of these stimuli upon us, through keeping our awareness on the experiential level, which for the sake of brevity, I will call "observation."

What does observation do?

Observation halts activity, because observation does not permit action. One has to pause in order to listen attentively; it is not possible to direct attention to both listening and to action at the same time. When an individual is active, his mind is distracted, and he does not listen. For a man to be able to receive information, he must cease all action. Action impairs his ability to perceive what is going on around him, while observation obligates man to stop being distracted by doing things. Should a classroom teacher notice a student being distracted by doing other things, he will point this out to the student, and ask him to pay attention and listen, because those distracted by doing are not free to listen or observe. Just as doing distracts us from attentiveness, attentiveness distracts us from doing. It therefore follows that if we want to cease doing, we need to sink into observation. This is the only technique we have available to reach a state of non-doing.

When we sink into attentiveness or observation, we

are actually immersing ourselves in the experience we are having here and now.

This experience does not take place in the past, or in the future, the experience only takes place in the present, at this moment! Hence it is common to define meditation as directing one's attention to the experience of this moment.

What have we gained by non-doing?

A state of non-doing ends responses to stimulation, because any response to stimulation is actually an action undertaken to achieve more pleasure or less pain. Such an action is a purpose-oriented action – it makes us focus on the thing we are trying to achieve, and it is precisely this focus that is the problem. The focus is the problematic part of the response to stimulation, for that is what drives us to distraction. What is focus? Focus is the concentration of our attention at a single point, which takes out of focus everything surrounding that point. When you are only focused on one thing, your mind is distracted from all other things around it. In meditation, we seek to reach a state of awareness, which is a state where consciousness expands to occupy areas that were formally the domain of the subconscious. The circle of attention expands more and more, until the boundary between the conscious mind and the subconscious mind is completely eliminated. The boundary between consciousness and subconsciousness is generated to begin with, precisely because of the focusing of attention on the single object we seek to concentrate on, and being distracted from everything else. This is what we want to stop! Focus is the most primordial expression of desire. The elimination of focus is in fact the elimination of desire, and the acceptance of reality as it is.

What happens to the consciousness when the circle of awareness expands?

Many good things happen when the circle of awareness expands. As the conscious portion of the mind expands to encompass more and more of the subconscious, our repressions, bound and concealed in the subconscious, rise up to the threshold of consciousness, and a process of catharsis, which heals the soul, begins. True, this process must be performed carefully and gradually. Releasing that which has been imprisoned by the subconscious all at once can lead to loss of mental equilibrium. However, the very process is one of healing, since it is repressions which are the cause of our stress. Since we repress that which we do not want to confront or to accept, we are in a constant state of flight from them. To ignore that which we repress, we must engage in constant distractions in order to avoid seeing them, and this is exhausting. The effort invested in repression drains our mental reserves.

When repression falters, and what is repressed rises to the threshold of consciousness, then the process of acceptance begins, and with it much of the tension pent up in the nervous system is released. We become calmer and our relationships with other people, and the world at large, improve. And then, as the tension dissipates, anger releases us as well and we become more compassionate, more understanding, and feel our unity with the world and all of its living things. A self-sustaining love that is not dependent on anything begins to radiate out of us, and suddenly our eyes open up to see how beautiful the world is, and the heart expands with joy. Another clear benefit we derive from meditation and the awareness it brings is "inspiration."

What is inspiration?

Inspiration is an idea popping into our head with no hint of where it came from. There is knowledge we acquire through deduction and induction of conclusions from what is clearly visible. This is called intelligence. As is said in Ecclesiastes: "The wise man has eyes in his head." And as the sages of Jewish tradition said: "Who is wise? He who sees what is to come." But this knowledge is the fruit of the thought of the wise. It is the correct thinking by the wise that lead them to reach the correct conclusions and thereby know things that other do not.

Inspiration is an entirely different source of knowledge. Inspiration is the useful "tips" you receive from above, not by the power of your own thought, just as a prophet receives knowledge of many things not by his own power, but from a spirit from above who speaks through him. The sages say: "better a wise man than a prophet," for wisdom is an innate quality of the wise man, whereas the spirit of prophecy comes and goes from the prophet. Some knowledge however cannot be arrived at without external help, so a wise man who is also a prophet is better than someone who is merely wise. Indeed, prophecy forms the basis of all religions. (See more concerning prophecy in appendix B.)

Why does meditation lead to inspiration? I thought about a beautiful proverb. When do the waters of the lake reflect the clouds in the sky? – when there is no wind, and the lake is calm and clear of any waves! So it is that thought, when it quiets down, becomes a mirror that reflects knowledge from the outside. Suddenly, thoughts pop up in your mind which you did not create with your own thinking. They pop up out of nowhere, since your mind has become a receptacle for thoughts from the outside, after it has stopped emitting thoughts outwards, for those occupied in emitting are not open to receiving.

Observation leads to self-awareness

Another benefit we can derive from observation is our ability to differentiate between that which is part of us and that which is outside of us. I call this differentiation ability "self-awareness." Observation sharpens in us the understanding that the object of observation is something external to us. When we observe something, observation in and of itself leads us to the understanding that this thing is not a part of us, for after all, one cannot observe anything except from an external vantage point.

This is why the observation of sensations is a very effective meditative technique. The sensations are a powerful observational object, for when we observe them, we are forced to acknowledge that they are not truly part of us. What are the sensations if not stimuli provided by our nervous system? As we have already explained, stimuli is the root of the problem, for they are what push us to respond and take action. When a disconnect is formed between the observer and the sensations he experiences, and the understanding that these sensations are not part of his self, his identification with these sensations ends, and thus his automatic response to stimuli ends. Then comes the calmness, the rest, and the self-content.

The separation and distance from the stimuli, which the observation of the sensations generates, ends the compulsive response to stimuli. Suddenly, instead of responding automatically, you find yourself stopping and asking yourself – who is forcing me to respond? Why must I enslave myself to the pursuit of pleasure? I am the master of my own soul! What reason do I have for discontent in the peaceful place where I now am? Why must I continue to pursue and be swept after momentary pleasures that come and go and are not a part of me? It is better to abolish desire, instead of constantly toiling in an endless attempt to satisfy it. Desire is never satiated, after all, and even if one does manage to momentarily sate it, it is soon rekindled to demand more and more. In contrast, the inner peace that remains when the stimuli are denied entry is sweeter than honey – and there is no need to strain oneself on its account.

Meta-cognition: an important byproduct of meditation

Have you ever heard of the term meta-cognition? Meta-cognition is the awareness of thoughts, and it too is a byproduct of meditation. One of the most effective meditation techniques is observing thoughts. Any observation leads toward the phenomena known as "meditation," regardless of the object one chooses to observe. However, the observed object does influence the meditational byproduct.

Most people are usually not aware of their own thoughts and let them flow freely. When you use thoughts running through your head as an object to observe, this obviously results in a cessation of activity, just like any time one is observing something. However, there is an added benefit – you learn to identify your own thought patterns.

We are usually not used to investigating our own thought patterns. Thought is so close to us that we tend to overlook it, seeing only what lies beyond it. It is just like we never see our own eyeglasses, which are too close to our eyes for us to notice, even though we observe the entire world through them. But if we fail to examine these windows, we cannot see the stains on the windowpanes, which distort the image and interfere with our perception.

Meditation makes us notice the gap between what is you and the many other things you tend to identify with as if they were you, since they are very close to you, but they are not really you – only tools you use. One of those tools is your thoughts. Meditation generates emotional separation between you and thought, and this separation enables you to disconnect from the control thought has over you. This is not control of thought – control is not meditation – but release of the grip thoughts have over you. Through this, you learn your own thought paths, and cease thinking automatically and subconsciously. Being aware of thinking is the field called "meta-cognition." I will later expand on meta-cognition.

Additional tips to help in the practice of meditation

An environment without many stimuli helps in the practice of meditation. For instance, sitting in a quiet place is something that will help considerably. Sitting out in the wilderness, far from the din of human settlements, is even better. Practicing in an isolated spot without any people is fine. Even if you don't have the option of staking out a spot in the great outdoors, and you decide to meditate at home, you need to select a quiet room without any people in it. It is not only your own thoughts that interfere with securing any inner peace, the thoughts of other people also influence your thoughts and will prevent you from silencing your thoughts. All of us are tied together in hidden ways.

Similar to reducing the level of stimuli from the environment, there are also ways to reduce the sensory stimulation threshold of the nervous system, which reduces the effect of stimuli on us. How is this done? You provide the nervous system with a powerful stimulus, and this reduces its sensory stimulation threshold. One way of doing so, is bathing in cold water. These tips can help you prepare a pleasant work environment which will ease the practice of meditation.

Spiritual assets that accumulate over time

The more one progresses in the spiritual journey of meditation, the more the stress level accumulated in the nervous system decreases, and the more this moderates human behavior, as one's traits become purer. Desire and ego no longer rule.

The intelligence of the meditating individual also increases with prolonged practice, as he connects to higher realms of intelligence, and his problem-solving capabilities rise as well.

Observation is a technique that allows awareness to occur

Some define meditation as "attentiveness," whereas others define it as "observation." It does not matter. Whether you call it observation or attentiveness, the final result of either is to place yourself in a state of awareness. Attentiveness or observation is merely an intermediate step leading to reducing activity and a state of awareness.

Observation interferes with activity and hence halts it. One cannot be simultaneously engaged in listening and taking action. A man busy doing is distracted and finds it hard to notice what is occurring around him. Oftentimes we will see how an individual takes a break from his frenzied activities in order to listen or observe attentively. Observation turns off activity, and activity turns off observation.

In meditation, instead of responding to stimuli, you observe it. In this way, the feedback loop of stimulus-response is halted and activity abates, and in the calm that is created, awareness develops on its own. The soil from which awareness grows is the quiet. In meditation, we do not create awareness – awareness happens on its own when the activity of the body and mind abates. Halting the activity is a precondition for entering a state of awareness. The moment activity abates, the conscious state of awareness begins to form. Entering the hall of awareness is blocked by multiple distractions. These distractions are not the stimuli themselves, but our responses to them. Exposure to the seductive stimuli can be reduced but cannot be completely eliminated. What can be eliminated is the habit of responding to them. Halting response to stimuli soothes activity and enables entry into a state of awareness.

Engaging in observation is like taking one step back in order to see things from afar. Out of this observation, one learns to acknowledge the separation between the observer and the observed object, and thereby grow to know the observer. The observation of which we speak is not like the observation of a man watching a movie – an observation characterized by concentration and identification leading him to totally immerse himself in the movie and be distracted from anything outside of it. That is not the observation we aspire to. Rather, we aim to observe at a distance, the observation of a bystander, one that disconnects from the observed object and which leads you to see yourself – the viewer – and recognize that you are disconnected from the observed object and need not respond to it automatically. This is not an active observation that requires effort and concentration, but a passive, restful, calm and non-involved observation.

The difference between concentration and awareness

Awareness is the diametrical opposite of concentration. When we focus on a specific spot, we distract ourselves from everything else, and distraction is the opposite of awareness. Hence, concentration does not bring us closer to awareness, but pushes us farther away from this state. A common proverb says: the fish cannot see the hook, since he is focused on the bait. Hypnosis is what requires concentration, not meditation. In hypnosis, the hypnotist brings the hypnotized to a state of extreme concentration, in order to enable the subconscious mind to take control, for it comes into play when an individual is in a state of distraction. The subconscious mind executes the fixed, automatic patterns that have been seared into it over time. Concentration created the boundary between the conscious and the subconscious by focusing the circle of attention into the limited area that is the conscious part, whereas everything else becomes the subconscious part, a part where other rules apply.

Meditation does the exact opposite. It brings to the surface, to consciousness, everything that has been repressed, and whatever conditioning has been imprinted in us, no longer controls our actions. Meditation expands our circle of attention so far, that the boundary between the conscious and the subconscious is abolished, and all that was locked up in the subconscious is released, resulting in significant relief, for repression takes up considerable mental effort and generates a lot stress.

At the end of the day the purpose of practicing meditation is to know thyself! That means being aware of the observer in you, which is the only thing that is actually you. All the rest is external, and not a part of you. Anything which can be observed is by definition not the observer. The very fact that you are observing something reveals that thing as something separate from you. Your identities are not a part of you; your sensations are not a part of you; your thoughts are not a part of you, and certainly external events are not a part of you. Hence there is no reason for you to identify with them, or to respond to them on autopilot.

There are many thought patterns which sour our mood and impair our quality of life without bringing us any attendant benefits. There are also thought patterns which actively harm us. Why then do we continue to compulsively run them through our mind? The choice is ours – we can take part in the thought process occurring within us, or we can choose not to partake and let it pass us by, without influencing us.

An observer who is not involved in what he watches – that is the sort of observation we are aiming for. To be purely an observer, without being an active participant in the play he is watching, not even as a judge deciding what is right and what is wrong – pure observation free of any judgement. Any action can only obscure one's awareness, for any action requires concentration, and concentration can only be achieved at the expense of awareness. When you focus on only one thing, you grow distracted from all other things. For instance: if you are listening to a lecture, and during the lecture you take notes of important points in order to remember them, it is only to be expected that you miss out whatever is said while you are taking notes, for listening and acting cannot be performed simultaneously. If you are occupied in doing, you cannot at the same time be attentive to what is being said in the lecture, for doing requires you to concentrate on a single thing – the purpose you wish to achieve through the action you are undertaking.

One of the indications that you are observing in the wrong way is that you are putting forth effort. Action requires effort. Rest requires no effort, so why are you making an effort? You cannot halt the stimulations and the thoughts and the sensations by force over time, and it is seemingly of no benefit to do so, for the moment they return, you are swept away in their wake. One can only secrete them outwards. It is observation that generates this secretion, which generates the disconnect. Observing something disconnects you from it, for it is not possible to observe it unless you are exterior to it. Thus, when you observe a noise taking place within – thoughts, emotions and sensations – observation in and of itself secretes this noise outwards and all that remains inwards is only the blessed silence which enables awareness to arrive, and it will arrive, for it is the natural state of consciousness. It is important to note that not every action requires concentration. An intuitive, spontaneous action does not lead to distraction, and hence does not reduce awareness. Only actions requiring thought, planning and choice demand concentration – for they are driven by an interest that, by definition, is a purpose to be achieved.

• • •

The course that we will study in this manual is composed of six lessons that are divided into three days, two lessons every day. All you need to do is to implement the instructions written in this manual, according to the order in which they are written. Should you operate according to the instructions, by the end of the three days, you will already know how to practice meditation in a basic manner. Of course, over time, your knowledge will grow and deepen the more experience you accumulate.

No changes in your lifestyle will be required beyond two 15–20 minute exercises, refreshing and effortless, every day. You will begin feeling the positive results sooner or later, depending on the individual. Some people will begin to feel a positive impact on day one; for others, the benefits will only be perceptible after a week or two, possibly even longer. For some people, the impact is powerful, whereas for others it is more gradual. But the eventual impact is certain – so long as you read this manual attentively and meticulously follow its instructions.

META-COGNITION

Thoughts about Thoughts

Being aware of thoughts is the ability to think about thoughts, what is termed in cognitive psychology "meta-cognition." Wikipedia defines it as follows: "**Metacognition** is an awareness of one's thought processes and an understanding of the patterns behind them. The root word *meta* means "beyond," or "on top of." Metacognition can take many forms, such as reflecting on one's ways of thinking and knowing when and how to use particular strategies for problem-solving."

Meta-cognition represents an individual's ability to explore his thoughts. All wisdom is based on a given method of inquiry, be it philosophy or science. The scientific methods of inquiry are different than the philosophical methods of inquiry and therefore lead to different conclusions. Has anyone ever thought of studying the methods of inquiry themselves in order to find out which method is best and leads to the most accurate conclusions, and which is wrong?

Greek philosophers believed that proofs could not be derived from the senses, because the senses can be fooled. Hence, they cannot be relied upon. For truth, one must rely on reason, so they claimed. Hence, all the philosophical insights, and even sciences like the Euclidean geometry, derived from Ancient Greece, begin with several simple assumptions ("first ideas") which the ancient Greeks called "axioms." They were the bases for the deduction of conclusions which they called "proofs."

I have heard that Aristotle claimed that women have fewer teeth than men. In reality, women have the same number of teeth as men. When Aristotle was married, why did he not simply ask his wife to open her mouth so he could count her teeth? But the convention among the Greek philosophers was not to present evidence derived from the senses. There was a method here which stated: one does not arrive at the truth through the senses but through the mind ("ideas").

This method of inquiry does not lead to the truth. Indeed, it leads the researcher to the conclusion that there is no truth, for what constitutes a "primary idea" or "axiom" in the eyes of one philosopher does not necessarily constitute an axiom to another philosopher, and in any event the conclusions derived by the first philosopher might be different, even contradictory, to those of the second philosopher. This situation, in which both one thing and the opposite can be proved, has undermined the faith in our ability, as human beings, to advance in the inquiry of the truth, and even undermine the very existence of the truth.

There was also a school of Greek Philosophers called the "sophists." They would prove to their audiences one argument on one day, and the very next day prove to the same audience the exact opposite, in order to show everyone that there is no truth. Many of the sophists were then persecuted. They were accused of disrespecting the gods and corrupting the youth.

Our senses are the only source of information we have in regard to what is occurring in the external world, but you need to know how to cross-reference the data that is received from different sources in order to verify it, which is known as "the scientific method." Science made a great step forward by changing the methods of inquiry that have been acceptable in the past. Of course, not everything that is published in the media in the name of science is actually scientific, but this is another topic. True, even in science, in the study of small particles from which matter is constituted, it turns out that it is seemingly possible for two opposites to be factually true. (See a discussion of this question in appendix A.)

A large part of the Talmud is dedicated to clarifying the correct methods of inquiry, that which is called in Halakhic literature "doubt resolution laws," which are instructions concerning the mode of action to be taken in situations of uncertainty.

In this manual, the occasional incorporation of metacognitive insights is that, as explained above, meditation and metacognition are tightly linked to one another. Even though metacognition is not meditation, it is a side benefit of meditation. In meditation, you observe thoughts in order to see the observer in you – yourself. In contrast, with metacognition, you are observing thoughts in order to see the thoughts themselves and be aware of them, and not give them control over you – but without trying to control them, otherwise it is no longer the observation of a bystander, and you lose awareness.

MEDITATION — GUIDANCE

Special cases

Medication and drugs, onion and garlic

According to Indian tradition, a man who eats garlic and onions finds it hard to reach higher degrees of awareness, since such foods tantalize the senses and prevent the calm disconnection from the stimulation of the senses. This is also true with regard to drinking alcohol or using drugs or pain killers.

If you are using light drugs or common drugs such as marijuana, you need to stop using them for at least 15 days prior to implementing the first lesson in this manual. Studies show that there is a need for a break of a minimum of 15 days in order to clear out the leftover marijuana from the body. If you are not willing to forsake the marijuana, then stop for as long as you can, and only then start studying the manual.

As for drinking alcohol, it has a shorter period of impact, lasting for only a few hours usually (depending on the amount). The same applies to common pain killers, tobacco, coffee and other such substances. Nonetheless, they all interfere with reaching gentle and subtle levels of awareness, and hence their use must be avoided in close proximity to the meditation practice.

Over time, those who regularly practice meditation tend to naturally and effortlessly reduce their use of distracting substances, since they learn to enjoy the experience of life itself, rather than seeking ways of escaping it.

Psychological difficulties

People who have suffered trauma may experience difficulty in practicing meditation, and it is recommended they perform shorter exercises, at least in the beginning. An individual who has suffered trauma cannot always deal with it when it is still fresh, and it is best to leave it repressed and wait for the right moment whereby the consciousness is capable of accepting it. When the trauma is too fresh to be floated to the surface of consciousness and be accepted, it is better to distract oneself from it and leave it repressed. If time has passed, and the soul is prepared to deal with the trauma, this is the proper time to raise it to the consciousness.

Meditation is a practice that brings to the surface that which has been suppressed, and in the initial stages when things rise to the surface, any individual might feel discomfort. You need to realize that these are the initial stages in which the wound opens up and the pus begins to drain away. It is all part of the soul's healing process. It will be followed by other stages in which you will feel the contentment and serenity that awareness brings.

People suffering from mental illnesses may undergo difficult psychological perturbations while practicing meditation, when that which has been suppressed begins to rise to the surface, and issues which can only be fully healed or addressed over a long period of time begin to prematurely reawaken.

If you suffered from harsh trauma at a young age, or you have been diagnosed with a mental illness in the past, or you suffer from chronic headaches, or you suffer from severe insomnia or other severe conditions, whether or not they have been diagnosed and treated by doctors, it is recommended you not practice meditation for more than 10 minutes at a time, so as to avoid the possibility that this problem re-emerge.

Even mentally healthy people, if they have accumulated a great deal of stress, may feel discomfort during the meditation practice. A sudden release of powerful stress, within a short period of time, may result in a feeling of fatigue, irritation, and a feeling of discomfort throughout the body. These complications can also be resolved by reducing the length of the meditation session, at least in the beginning.

META-COGNITION

The cause, the record and what lies between

Truth is not a story one individual can share with another via words. Words are too small to contain the truth. Words can have more than one meaning, and besides, the invention of language also introduced lies to the world. Truth is something each and every individual should go out and seek for himself. The tools to seek out the truth can and should be given to an individual but using them to find truth is a task that must be left to him. Clearly every individual needs good teachers, but he should learn insights from them, not accept their teachings blindly, with no verification and no inquiry of his-own.

With what shovel can the precious ore called "truth" be mined from the earth?

What tool should a man use when seeking out truth?

That tool is evidence.

What is evidence?

Evidence is composed of four parts:
1. The cause
2. The effect

3. The trace
4. The record

Let us illustrate this through an example:
An explosion has generated a crater in the ground. You do not need to see the explosion to know a bomb went off. It is enough to see the crater left behind by the explosion to know a bomb went off. This knowledge does not depend on understanding how and when the bomb went off here of all places. It is self-supporting knowledge. It is clear as rain that the bomb went off, even if we did not see it explode, since the explosion left a trace in the ground. And even though we did not see the explosion, we can see the crater generated by the explosion and that is equivalent to seeing the explosion itself with our eyes. Actually, it is more significant than witnessing it. Seeing the explosion would only show us the thing itself, whereas the crater indicates the impact of the explosion on some other object, which is a validation and confirmation in practice of its existence. Eyesight in and of itself is not something that can be relied upon, because the senses can be fooled.

In this example, the cause is the bomb, whereas the effect is the explosion. The bomb and the explosion it caused were not witnessed by us, they were in the past and they are gone. Nonetheless, we know they occurred, with certainty, because of the trace (the crater) left by the explosion in the ground, which constitutes the record. Phrased differently, evidence is knowing that which we cannot see, due to the trace it left on something else, which we can see.

Another example:
A fingerprint is evidence that the individual whose fingerprint is present came into contact with this surface at some point. The finger is the cause. Its contact with the surface is the effect. The fingerprint is the trace, and the surface on which the fingerprint was imprinted is the record.

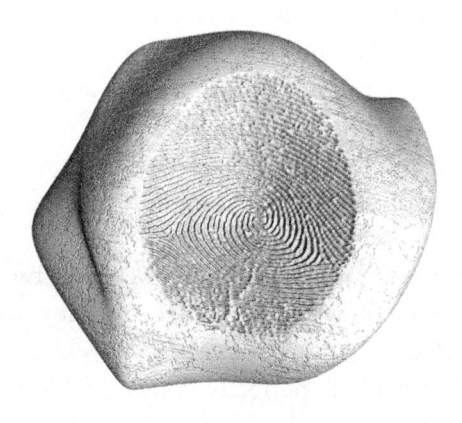

This does not prove, of course, that, in the case of a police investigation, the person who was present at the location carried out the crime being investigated. That is an assumption rather than a fact. It is important to know how to distinguish between evidence and assumptions. So long as no evidence has been found to clarify the truth, we make presumptions that define how we choose to act, for now, until the truth is clarified, for the world does not pause even when there is uncertainty, and even in a time of uncertainty, one must sometimes decide what action to take in the meantime until evidence is found that determines the truth.

In the Talmud, presumption is called *hazakah*, a term linguistically derived from the Hebrew word for holding (*lehahzik*), for it is the truth we hold in our minds, until proven otherwise. Given that one of the most fundamental presumptions is that a man is presumed innocent so long as he is not proven guilty, punishment demands evidence. According to the Talmud, a prohibition can be placed on the basis of a hazakah – that is, without clear evidence – but not a punishment. In order to levy a punishment, clear evidence that one has transgressed against the prohibition is required.

According to the Talmud, a testimony by two witnesses constitutes evidence, according to the same principle of evidence explained above:

You cross-reference information between two sources, in this case two witnesses who claim they saw a given event. Had they not both seen the event, then their stories are unlikely to perfectly match up, for a man inventing a story out of thin air is unlikely to include the same details that another person doing the same, came up with – at least when there is no possibility for the two sources colluding and coordinating their story.

But what if there was such collusion between the two sources? Or that both sources relied on a single, third, source?

When both witnesses provide identical versions, cross-referencing their testimonies does not constitute evidence. By the nature of things, different witnesses will tend to see the same event from somewhat different perspectives, and notice different details, so their versions of an event cannot be identical, but rather complementary.

How they line up needs to be like how two parts of a puzzle match up – when coming together, they complete the same picture, but they are not identical to one another.

There is a tale of a man and woman who were accused of adultery. Two witnesses testified that they saw them formicating. The man and the woman wept before the Rabbi and claimed that no such thing had taken place. The Rabbi was embarrassed. On the one hand, he was obligated to accept the veracity of two witnesses whose testimony was found to match up even in small details, but on the other hand, the weeping of the two defendants seemed very authentic. What was to be done?

The Rabbi forwarded the question to the Vilna Gaon. The Gaon Rabbi Eliyahu sat down and heard the versions of the witnesses and then yelled at them "Liars! Admit you are bearing false witness!" The witnesses were frightened and confessed. The Rabbi who directed the question to the Gaon wondered at how he knew that the witnesses were liars, as their stories matched up completely. The Gaon told him: when two witnesses recount the exact same story, there is no doubt that they coordinated their testimonies. A cross-referencing that constitutes valid evidence is one where the two stories complete each other, not when they are identical to one another.

For a cross-reference to constitute evidence, the person questioning the witnesses needs to be alert and an expert in his profession, lest errors occur. But such failures are not the result of a flaw in the two-witness testimony tool to inquire after the truth, but rather the result of the absence of investigator skill to make proper use of it.

• • •

The First Temple contained, in its Holy of Holies, the Ark of the Covenant, also called the Ark of the Testimony, which housed the stone tablets testifying to the covenant between the People of Israel and their heavenly Father. Above the lid of the Ark of the Covenant were two cherubs (angelic figures in the form of golden infants), one male and one female, who gazed at one another. What were the two cherubs hinting at? What is the relation between male and female? Male is the giver and the female the receiver, like the moon which lacks its own light, that is precisely what enables it to reflect the light of the sun. We cannot see the sun in the darkness of the night, but out of its light, reflected in the moon, we can know of its existence even in the absence of direct sight. Rabbi Abulafia interprets the image of the cherubs in his book "Life in the World to Come" as follows:

"... and indeed, the two cherubs are there to hint at the divine presence and they represent cause and effect – male and female, hence they (the cherubs) are united in a single body with two forms, and they gaze at one another, with the holy name of God present between them. (Rabbi Abraham Abulafia, in his book "Life in the World to Come").

**The Ark of the Covenant placed on the
Foundation Stone in the Temple of Jerusalem**

MEDITATION — GUIDANCE

Pre-Exercise 1 Questionnaire

Before starting with your first exercise, please fill out the questionnaire below. This is a questionnaire concerning your current quality of life. By filling it out now, you will be able to revisit it after you begin practicing meditation, compare the answers, and observe possible improvements. The questionnaire is intended to examine symptoms of stress, and you should rank each symptom in accordance with the level you experience it. Check the appropriate box, from 1 to 10. If you do not experience the symptom at all, check the 0 column.

Question	0	1	2	3	4	5	6	7	8	9	10
I feel nervous											
I sense anxiety											
I find it hard to fall asleep at night											
My sleep is interrupted											
I have nightmares											
I suffer from headaches											
I often feel sad											
I am not satisfied with my life											
I am not happy											
My mind is sleepy											
I constantly worry											
I am obsessive											
My thoughts are troubled											
I forget things											
I have no self confidence											
I feel uncomfortable around other people											

I am often sick											
I seem older than my age											
My intelligence is low											
My intuition is weak											
I suffer from high blood pressure											
I smoke too many cigarettes											
I drink too much alcohol											
I often bite my nails											
I suffer from nervous tics											
I use too many sedatives or recreational drugs											
I am addicted to drugs or alcohol											
I suffer from anxiety attacks											
I take too many over-the-counter medications											
I am afraid of the dark											
I fear death											

Exercise 1

Reserve at least half an hour for yourself to perform the first exercise. The length of the exercise is 15 minutes, but give yourself more time, so everything should be done calmly, with no pressure. Let us think for a moment on what meditation is. Meditation is doing nothing. When activity gives way to silence, awareness occurs on its own. How much effort does it take to do nothing? If you are putting in effort, that is one of the clearest signs you are not performing the meditation correctly. Meditation is simply sitting on a chair comfortably and just *being*, not doing anything, just being a passive viewer. Anything requiring effort is doing, and any doing is noise distracting one's mind and interfering with being aware. Awareness is not something you do; it takes place on its own when you stop doing things. The exercise helps us achieve inner peace, but awareness occurs on its own.

That is why it is good to start meditation with a few minutes of absolute silence, without practicing anything, just sitting silently. This is so that the exercise can begin from an attitude of non-doing. The natural tendency of anyone not experienced in meditation, is to immediately, as soon as the exercise begins, start troubling their mind with all sorts of questions: What should I do? What should I observe? Breathing? Thoughts? Should I begin reciting the mantra? Don't be concerned about the practice of meditation, for it is not actually possible to practice meditation, as it does not involve any doing. It is non-doing. In order to silence any activity occurring within us, such as the activities of thought, we use methods which take us closest to a state of non-doing, so we can skip from there easily to the utter silence that enables awareness to take place. A few minutes of silence in the beginning of meditation puts us in the right state of mind, the right attitude – an attitude of non-doing.

It is important to also end the meditation with a few minutes of silence in which you do not observe, and do not repeat the word, only sit in utter silence, to give your consciousness the time it needs to gradually leave the pure state of awareness and return to a normal state of mind. When you meditate, you open a portal to a higher plane. When you leave it, close the portal behind you! Experienced meditators say that it eases the return to this state the next time around. Nor is it good to suddenly shock the nervous system, after a long period of serenity.

How to sit during meditation

When we sit without doing anything, especially for the first time, our head is filled with thoughts. Many people are basically addicted to intensive activity and must constantly keep themselves occupied since this is a form of escape – a distraction from things we do not want to think about. When you experience the silence of non-doing for the first time, the thoughts we have fled from all these years can rise up and flood the consciousness as all that was repressed over the years float back up to the surface. That can result in a very unpleasant feeling. But there is no need to be alarmed, this is a process of purification. Meditation returns us to awareness and teaches us to accept instead of repress. This transition releases the nervous system from many pressures that have accumulated in it over the years.

The nervous system is where stress accumulates. The neural fibers making up the nervous system begin in the brain, descend through the spinal cord, and from there spread to the various organs. The nerve endings are at the tips of the hands and feet, beneath our nails, and that is where most of the stress is accumulated. These tensions drain the body of energy and resources. Stress leads the body to produces certain types of hormones and other chemical substances that help it deal with situations of threat and danger, but drains the body's energy, and over time wear the body down. There are various approaches to release tension from the nervous system. One of them is Reflexology. Reflexology is the massage of the nerves, particularly at their tips, in order to relieve them of tension. When tension is released, the blood vessels open up, blood flow increases, and the organs receive plentiful oxygen and nutrition. The cells of the immune system reach the organs in greater numbers, by the increased blood flow, and thus the body heals itself.

Meditation also releases tension from the nervous system. The spinal column is an important component of the nervous system, and a large portion of the neural energy passes through it. When the spinal cord is straight, it is easier for energy to flow through it, which is why it is better to practice meditation when you are sitting up straight, so that your spinal cord is straight and the energy flows through it easily. This does not mean you need to make an effort to keep your back straight – effort and meditation do not mix. But you do need to keep a proper posture of your spinal column. Led your head lean slightly backwards, so that the first vertebrae between the neck and the head is at the proper angle – slightly tilted backwards. Tilt the pelvis forward so that the final vertebrae connecting to the pelvis will be oriented at the proper angle – tilted forward. Now, once the first and final vertebrae are at the proper angle, the other vertebrae are oriented on their own in their natural and correct form, and an erect posture is achieved with no effort. There is no need to entwine your legs in a painful lotus posture, for this is of no benefit to most people. You can sit comfortably on a chair, with your legs straight ahead. Those who find it difficult to keep their back straight, can lean backwards using the headrest, but at least try to keep your neck held up straight, though not stiffly.

You need to position your thighs on the chair so that the pressure will not be focused solely on the buttocks. When you tilt the pelvis forward the body weight naturally falls on the thighs as well, and so the pressure is spread over a large area, and sitting over time does not hurt. Find a comfortable chair which provides support – for the hips as well.

Meditation location

It is best to practice meditation somewhere quiet, outdoors. Quiet does not necessarily mean a place that is free of noises and voices alone. If you practice meditation in a home filled with people, even if everyone keeps quiet, the thought about the people present in the house generates turbulence which makes it difficult to achieve mental quiet. Hence, the outdoors are best. However, if this is not possible, seek out an isolated and closed room in the house, ideally one that is dimly lit. Experienced meditators can enter a state of full awareness in a noisy environment as well, but when you are starting out, it is better you look for a place that is as quiet as possible.

When should you practice meditation?

It is best to practice at regular intervals – a morning and evening practice. You should carry out the first exercise in the morning before starting your workday, and also before breakfast. You should not meditate close to meal time and certainly not after a full meal. The digestion process interrupts the silencing, and so you should wait for two hours after your meal before you practice meditation. Nor should you meditate before going to sleep. About two hours before sleep, the body's biological clock already puts you in a state of drowsiness, and hence you should schedule the meditation at least two hours before your bedtime.

What happens during the exercise?

During the exercise, you stop being the one doing the action, and you are no longer thinking actively; you merely watching the thoughts in your mind as they come and go, or watching any other activity that is happening within you.

You will notice that thought does not fall silent, even when you do not think about anything deliberately. How can it be that thought continues to be active, if you only watch it, and you are not the one initiating the activity?

These thoughts, which continue to emerge on their own, partially express a release of tension that emerges out of the subconsciousness (repression generates the tension, and when it is released, the tension decreases). Some are the inspiration we receive from above. This inspiration is expressed in ideas that help us to succeed in achieving our destiny or find solutions to problems and challenges which we encounter in our daily life. These thoughts arise because you no longer intervene in enforcing your will on the system, so it is free to calibrate itself and reach balance on its own.

Experienced meditators describe the process they undergo during meditation as being divided into two parts. The first part is called "the move inwards." In this stage, the process of quieting the inner activity through observation takes place. Instead of responding to stimuli, you simply observe them, and thereby the activity in response to stimuli, be they pain stimuli or pleasure stimuli, comes to an end. The storm of stimuli continues, only the responses end and have been replaced with observation. As soon as you start observing, you have removed yourself from the midst of the storm and have drawn away from it. It now continues to rage – but from afar. In the homely environment within yourself, there is quiet, the fireplace is burning, and it is warm and pleasant. With quiet comes the second stage of meditation: "the move outwards," in which awareness expands and a flow of thoughts arrives. These are thoughts that arise on their own. This flow of gripping thoughts is actually the process of recovery and return to the source, and it is necessary to open up and surrender to it when it arrives. The cycle of a move inwards and a move outwards can repeat itself several times during the exercise. When you notice one cycle has ended, you can begin another cycle of observation.

Exercise 1: Instructions

Basically, the exercise is to observe what we experience here and now, without thinking about what was or what will be. Observation is connecting attention to the experience. I am deliberately saying connection, rather than focusing. In meditation you don't let your thoughts distract you from the experience. But you are not supposed to focus on the experience and distract your mind from thoughts, and certainly not focus on the thoughts in order to hunt down every stray thought and forcefully terminate it. By doing so, you are merely empowering these thoughts with more attention. The way you should keep your attention engaged at the experiential level can be compared to a man driving his car on a rainy day. He keeps his eye on the road without letting the wipers, moving right and left before his eyes, distract him. He can see the road through their movement – and that is exactly how you should observe: by observing the experience **through** your thoughts.

What experience should you connect to? Whichever one you choose! You can listen to flowing water, a crackling fire, or even to the murmur of the air conditioner. I personally recommend being mindful of the sensations of the body, and especially to respiration. The air flowing through your nostrils as you breathe. Do not try to change your natural breathing rhythm, just feel it. The sensation of breathing is the most primordial experience man has when he emerges into the world. It is a very fine, gentle, experience, and it is easy to skip from it to awareness, which is where we are headed.

- Choose a comfortable time in the morning hours to begin the exercise.
- Select a quiet and secluded spot where you will not be disturbed.
- A place with dim lighting is preferable, at least for the first few times.
- A comfortable chair with a wide seat, on which one can rest the thighs.
- A clock you can occasionally glance at in order to get an idea of the length of the exercise. There is no need to be precise about the time, only to have a general idea of its passage. Meditation should not be subject to a schedule. Schedules have goals, and goals contradict the spirit of the exercise. A stopwatch generates anticipation and thoughts about when the alarm will

sound, and that does not enable you to immerse yourself in experiencing the moment, and hence it is best to avoid using one.
- You need to reduce the amount of external stimuli to a minimum, and hence you should close your eyes.
- When the time allotted to your exercise ends, sit for a little while longer without doing anything. Let your consciousness return to its regular state gradually.

Continue reading the manual until you reach the chapter heading "exercise number 2," and then pause. Read the instructions of exercise number two immediately prior to the second exercise, which should be this evening.

META-COGNITION

Physical evidence

There are hidden things that are not discernible to our eyes. Nonetheless, we know they exist because they leave their imprint on something else. Observation of this imprint is also seeing through our senses – the eye sees the reflection of the indiscernible entity on the discernible entity. We call this "physical evidence."

Physical evidence works much like a voice recording. It is actually an entity that serves as an audiotape recording the encounter with the indiscernible entity that left its imprint on it, thereby constituting evidence of the existence and nature of the indiscernible entity, provided that the imprinted body cannot generate this imprint on its own. This is because it is contrary to its nature, and the imprint is unique and typical only of the indiscernible entity, and cannot be replicated or forged.

In any encounter between two things that are very different from one another, if as a result of this encounter one of them left something unique of itself in its counterpart, that residue, that imprint, can constitute physical evidence that these two objects came into contact with one another at some point.

Definition of physical evidence:

Physical evidence is an entity that has been imprinted (that is bears traces, or an imprint) by the indiscernible entity, during their encounter, provided that:
1. This trace could not be manufactured by the trace bearing entity.
2. That the trace is unique to the indiscernible entity, which means it can only derive from a single source.

Examples:

An apple from which a bite has been taken. The bitten-out chunk is conspicuous as a trace which mars the wholeness of the apple and is contrary to its natural form, and the apple is incapable of manufacturing the bite on its own, so it must have come from an outside source and reflect the trace of some external factor. Any defect or deviance that is contrary to the character or natural fabric of the trace bearing body must be an imprint by an external factor. To discover who took a bite out of the apple, look for an individual whose bite leaves a unique imprint with an identical pattern to the chunk removed from the apple.

A shoeprint in the ground who shape is foreign to the texture of the ground. Clearly, some external entity left the shoeprint in the ground, and hence even if no shoe is found to precisely match the shoeprint and indentation, this constitutes physical evidence that a shoe with a pattern matching the shoeprints stepped on this spot at some point. If in addition the shoe sole has flaws and notches distinctive to it, setting it apart from all other shoes, then this constitutes a unique trace which serves as physical evidence for a specific shoe which can be searched for.

A fracture line on a plate fragment. The fracture line sharply bisects the circular shape of the plate, and is not a natural continuation of it, and so it is clear that the plate is marred and missing a part. Furthermore, the fault line is jagged and extremely complex and it is not possible that a precisely equivalent fault line was generated in some other broken plate. Therefore, should an additional plate fragment be found, with a precisely compatible fault line, this would constitute physical evidence that the second part found had originally been broken off of here and was originally attached to it, for you would have the two conditions required to constitute physical evidence.

A palm tree growing in the middle of a parched desert upon which rains never fall, constitutes physical evidence for the existence of a hidden source of water, which must be near where the tree flourishes. This is so even without any sensory evidence of the water. This is not merely completion of what is missing by the power of generalization, but the absence itself which broadcasts its existence by generating an unnatural change in the desert plain, a change that is readily apparent and that could not exist without the water source. Therefore you have the two conditions required to constitute physical evidence.

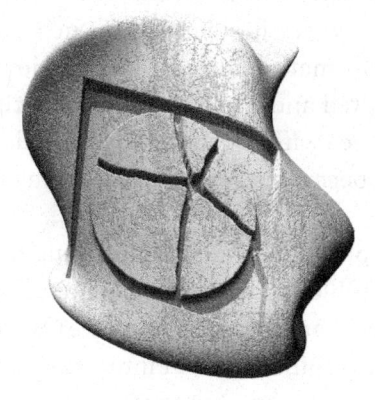

Another example of physical evidence is a matching of the material from which a piece has fallen, provided that the composition of the material is foreign to where it was found. For instance, every individual possesses unique DNA. DNA which has dropped onto an object constitutes evidence that the person possessing this DNA has touched this object at some point, or else stayed nearby (unless some third intermediary brought the DNA there).

Hence, the uniqueness of the trace, is not in its form, but in its material composition.

I have heard a claim that it is possible for two individuals to possess identical DNA, or DNA so similar that it is not possible to distinguish any difference between them, in a case of identical twins. In this case, a DNA test is not physical evidence, because a trace that is not unique to a specific source cannot be traced back to its origin, and hence it teaches us nothing and is of no use. Any guess we make concerning the entity that may have imprinted it is mere speculation, and the evidence does not necessitate its veracity. However, if the trace is unique, but we do not know where it stems from, such evidence contains new information for us – information that is currently encrypted and which we cannot decipher. This is called "evidence without context." Such evidence should be archived, because a source (donor) may be found for it one day.

There are pieces of evidence indicating the identity of the undiscernible, without revealing anything of its essence, and there are some that indicate the essence of the indiscernible (profile) without interpreting any identifying mark for it. One way or another, we always have to ask ourselves what the evidence clarifies for us and realize – it can only prove that which it clarifies. If at the end of the day, it is not clear what imprinted the evidence, or there is more than one possible source that could have generated it, then we are left in doubt, and nothing has actually been proven. True, if the evidence has ruled out some possibilities, then it should be archived, for perhaps some other piece of evidence will rule out other possibilities, and by cross-referencing both pieces of evidence, we will reach full clarification.

Let me tell you a story illustrating how important it is to always ask: What exactly does the evidence clarify? One night, a pistol shot was fired and shattered a streetlight. The police were able to locate the bullet which was embedded in the streetlight. The notches on the bullet indicate the pistol from which it was fired, since any barrel of a firearm has notches that are unique to it alone, as well as particles of discharge that have etched themselves into it over time, which scratch the bullet that is shot out of the barrel, leaving in it a trace unique to this barrel. If there is compatibility between the pattern of scratches on the bullet and the pattern of notches in the barrel, that poses physical evidence that this pistol is the firearm that shot this bullet, for the bullet cannot scratch itself, nor can it be manufactured with such scratches. However, such evidence does not prove that the owner of the pistol pulled the trigger. That is a generalization which states: for the most part, he who shoots the pistol is also its owner, but this is not absolute. Perhaps in this case, the son of the pistol owner took the gun without his father's permission or knowledge and played with it until a bullet was fired, damaging the streetlight? If this is the case, then the father can perhaps be accused of negligence, but not of inflicting the damage himself, because in this matter his guilt has not been proven, and any individual whose guilt has not been proven should enjoy the presumption of innocence.

Another example concerning this same matter, of asking ourselves what we know by evidence and what we assume by presumption: a man who claims that his friend never repaid a debt and holds a deed attesting to this. The deed the witnesses have signed, if a court of law investigated each separately and found their testimony compatible with one another, constitutes physical evidence that indeed there was a loan, and we have already explained why a two witness testimony constitutes physical evidence. But what exactly are the witnesses who have undersigned the deed testifying to? Only that a loan took place, not that it was never repaid! Should the borrower claim to have repaid his debt, he may well be telling the truth, but the burden of proof is on him, by power of the general rule that a creditor holding a deed is a creditor with an unpaid debt. After all, it is customary upon repayment for the borrower to repossess the deed to prevent a double collection, or else to collect a receipt from the creditor as proof of repayment.

A red car that collided into a blue car, leaving some of its paint on the blue car. Even without observing the accident, it is clear that the blue car underwent an accident, for it was not manufactured with red paint on it, and its form has been marred by some external factor which distorted its shape. Now the car that collided into it must be sought out based on the chemical match of its color to the trace found on the impacted vehicle, and whose shape matches the impact of the impacted vehicle. Should the trace be unique to a given vehicle, then this is physical evidence that proves which car impacted the blue car, but it is not physical evidence of the identity of the driver who caused the accident. Deciding that the owner of the car is also the driver at the time of the accident is an assumption based on generalization. There is no physical evidence for the individual responsible for the accident.

Any evidence that is not tangible evidence is in fact no more than a premise, a working assumption, but not actual evidence, for it is not based on direct sensory perception.

A fingerprint found at the scene of a crime constitutes evidence that the man possessing this fingerprint was at the scene at some time in the past. Fingerprints do not simply appear on objects out of nowhere, some external factor needs to imprint them on the object. Furthermore, their origin can only come from a single individual. Thus, we have all the components for a physical evidence. However, the knowledge concerning the presence of the owner of the fingerprint at the scene of the crime does not necessitate that it is he who committed the murder. To deduce from his presence at the scene that he was the one who committed the crime is not physical evidence.

Even when fingerprints found at the scene of the crime

are stained with the blood of the victim – which is physical evidence that he touched the victim while he was injured, this does not constitute physical evidence that he murdered the victim. Perhaps he tried to treat him when he was injured? Even should the weapon which injured the victim be identified, meaning that the nature of the unique injury inflicted by this weapon constitutes physical evidence that this weapon was used to commit the murder, and on this weapon fingerprints stained with the blood of the victim have been found, this too does not constitute physical evidence that the individual possessing this fingerprint committed the murder. Perhaps he touched the injured man with the best of intentions and got blood on his hands, and then picked up the weapon which was lying around at the scene?

Thus, a fingerprint is not a physical evidence enabling placement of responsibility on an individual for committing any act beyond the act of touching. A fingerprint is physical evidence indicative of the toucher, but in regard to the question of who committed the crime it is merely circumstantial evidence, which might render the owner of the fingerprint a suspect to be monitored, but not into a criminal worthy of punishment.

We have defined what constitutes evidence, now let us define what does not constitute evidence

To illustrate what does not constitutes evidence, let us begin with a story about two neighbors. Reuven and Simon are neighbors. Reuven one day comes to Simon with a grievance – "Your son hurled a rock at my window and broke it."

"Have you seen this with your own eyes?" Simon asks him.

"No, but I can bring you two witnesses who have seen it," answers Reuven.

"So what," says Simon. "I will bring you a hundred witnesses who saw nothing."

A funny answer, isn't it? Just because you can't see something, does not constitute evidence it is not there!

The lack of sensory input in the present cannot cancel out discovery once it has taken place. If a plane passes in front of a window, is visible, and then is gone, does that mean that the plane has ceased to exist? Of course not! The fact that it is now being obscured is merely the absence of discovery and hence proves nothing. Even a small glimpse of discovery removes a great deal of obscurement, just as a small light can repel much darkness. One brief moment of discovery can clarify to us an insight that even a thousand years of obscurity cannot blur.

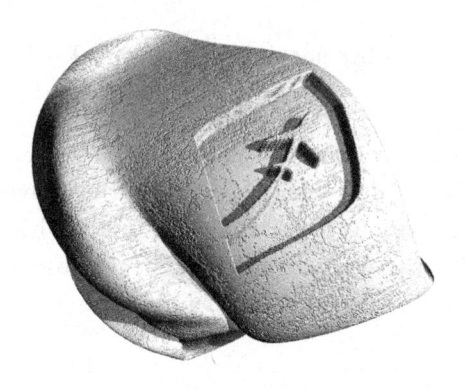

Absence therefore proves nothing. Some things can exist in the same room you are in, and your limited senses will not perceive them, such as bacteria or radio waves. But you nonetheless know they exist. The absence can be a result of obscurity, not of lack, and hence proves nothing. If we see a fish peeking out of murky water, we will know there is a fish in the pool. If immediately after discovery the fish dives back down to hide in the murky depths of the pool, shall we now say there is no fish in the pool? Of course not! Presence can prove existence, while seeming absence does not prove non-existence.

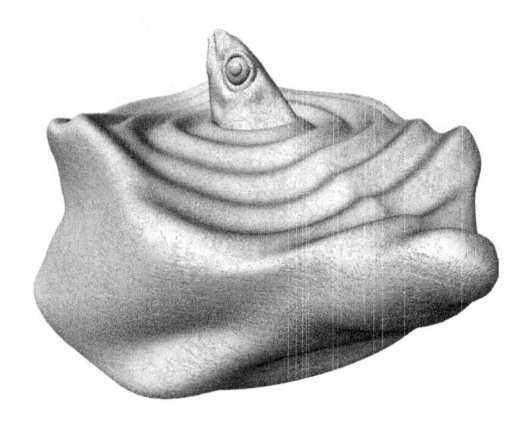

A fish peeking out of the pool

Even if you had sharp senses that could perceive everything, and nothing was hidden to your eyes, would it be possible for you to see all that was and will be throughout all times and places from the beginning of creation and to its end? Of course not, and hence non-existence cannot be proven.

Post-Exercise 1 Report

Please fill out the following report. The report is intended for your personal use, so that following the exercise you will spend some time observing the impact the exercise had on you. Make a checkmark next to the influences you felt during the exercise.

Report for exercise 1	Date and time:
Possible influence	Mark with checkmark
I felt calm	
The pace of my thoughts slowed down	
There were moments in which I had no thoughts at all	
I felt emotional discomfort	
I felt physical discomfort	
I felt stress relief	
I experienced involuntary movements	
Old memories were stirred	
I felt like smiling	
I felt inner peace	
At the end, I felt refreshed	

META-COGNITION

Seeing what is missing

In any research, one must occasionally use one's imagination, for example:

Aristotle claimed that rest was a natural and regular state and that every physical body aspires to it. In contrast, movement is a deviation from the natural state of a body, therefore it requires a casual explanation, because it must derive from external influence on the body.

The renowned physicist Isaac Newton disputed Aristotle's claim. He said that movement does not always require a casual explanation. For instance, in space, where there is no friction with air, a body which is in motion will continue moving forever, in the same direction and at the same speed, until some external force halts or diverts it from its course. Therefore it is more correct to say that the change from movement to rest and vice versa is what requires a casual explanation. Newton says that momentum is what is natural for the body and requires no explanation. The law of nature that constrains an object from changing its speed or its direction of movement is called the "law of conservation of momentum" and any object seemingly operating in conflict with this law and changes its speed or direction of movement, requires a casual explanation that will provide us with the data we require to complete the puzzle, which is: What is the external factor that influenced it to veer off course?

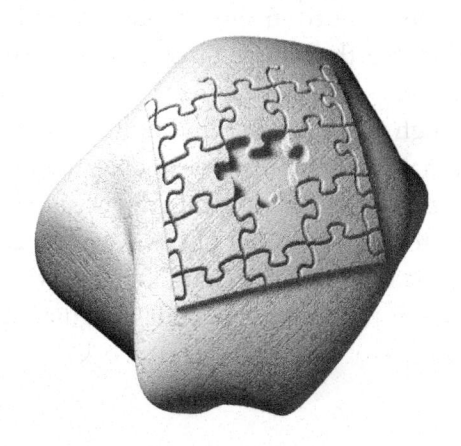

Something is missing

Newton did not dispute Aristotle on a fundamental level. He too admitted that deviation from natural normalcy requires a casual reason. He differed merely in claiming that inertia is the natural state and that deviation off course, or a change of speed, is the deviation indicating a trace of some imperceivable external factor.

According to this principle, one can prove the existence of hidden causes without perceiving them by sight, if they have an influence on the straight course of a perceivable object, and this is one way to prove the existence of black holes, even though they themselves cannot be seen – the influence they have on the stars around them can be seen.

This chapter is about a different type of physical evidence. The usual kind of physical evidence leads us to seek out the source of the evidence – the entity that left traces behind. But there is nothing to look for in the cases that are mentioned in this chapter. There is nothing to be found, for the source of the traces is something imperceptible.

But though we will never find it, its existence is certain, for it has left behind its traces on something that is perceivable. This type of physical evidence is no less clear and absolute than any other physical evidence. The fact that it leaves room for imagination, doesn't mean that it leaves room for doubt. Use your imagination! That's what it's for!

Black holes

A galaxy is a massive cluster of stars, constantly revolving around a given center, but that center is, surprisingly, empty! Well, at least there is nothing visible there. This circular movement around what seems to be an empty void is seemingly in contradiction to the law of momentum conservation. Why do the stars not move in a straight line, as the law dictates? The break in this continuity is a trace constituting evidence that something does exists at the center of the galaxy and is leaving its trace on the stars around it, by exerting a powerful pull upon them, causing them to revolve around it, though it is miniscule in size compared to them and relative to its attractive force.

The pattern of the missing puzzle piece at the center

of the galaxy therefore exactly matches the characteristics of a black hole, which is a highly condensed substance, with massive gravitational force relative to its size, and imperceptible as it does not reflect light beams, but rather swallows them due to its massive gravity. This is therefore an example of physical evidence of a hidden cause, which we have never seen and never will see, but whose existence can nonetheless be proven by the seeming violation of the law of conservation of momentum. Sure, tracking down the cause of this seeming violation requires active use of imagination – but that is precisely what imagination exists for.

Air particles

Here is another example of physical evidence that proves the existence of an imperceptible factor, and therefore requires the use of imagination.

Air particles cannot be observed by the naked eye. These are very small and move very rapidly, which even the greatest magnifying devices cannot detect, but their influence on larger particles is readily apparent. Take for instance smoke particles – these are relatively large particles and can be observed with a sufficiently powerful microscope. When smoke particles are moving in the air, the impact of air particles on smoke particles can be observed, and as a result of this impact, the smoke particles cannot stop shaking. Thus, even though the air particles themselves cannot be perceived, their existence can be known by their influence on the smoke particles. Smoke particles are simple, and they have no quality which might generate this odd shaking movement. They are supposed to move upwards in a straight line, with the warm air current rising up from the fire. As this is behavior contrary to the law of the thing itself, one must seek its cause in an external factor, which is surely missing here, to complete the whole picture. This factor must be the air particles, which move rapidly, and impact and shake the smoke particles.

Fossils

The trace usually not merely proves the existence of its unobserved source, but teaches us something about its character. Sometimes, it is even possible to imagine how it appeared (at least partially) by the shape of the traces left by it on another object, just as one can learn about the animals that once lived from the fossils left in rock layers. One of the ways in which a fossil is formed is this: the rock is initially a soft sludge into which the animal sank. Then, over the years, this sludge solidifies into a solid rock and the body of the animal sinking into it decomposes and disappears. Once the rock layer solidifies, the shape of the body that sank into it is preserved, and this spatial pattern constitutes physical evidence of the past existence of the animal that vanished. One need not see the actual animal which left an imprint of its shape in the fossil in order to get some idea of what it looked like. The trace left in its wake leaves no room for doubt, and that is what informs us of its shape and to some extent its essence, even though nothing is left of it.

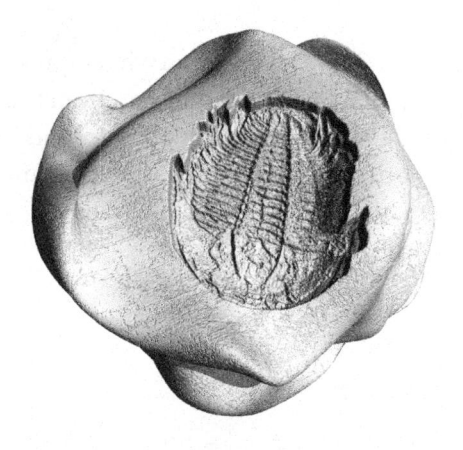

The shape of the fossil breaks up the continuity of the natural texture of the rock, which has no capacity to generate the foreign pattern of the shape it carries in it. Hence, it is clear that some external factor made the imprint. Now, all that is left to do is to examine the shape of the traces, and to try to derive from it information about the nature of that obscured factor that made the imprint – a factor which must perfectly match the shape of the impression and complete the absent material.

Some fossil shapes belong to animals who have never been observed by researchers, but nonetheless it is possible to extract considerable information from the shape they have left in the rock, for the trace contains many details which may shed some light on the qualities and characteristics of these animals, even though we have never directly observed them, and never will in the future, for no living specimens survived. The traces they have imprinted on other objects makes this possible and there is no need to perceive them with our senses, either in the past or the present. It is enough to know what is absent from the pattern the absence left on what is present when they came in contact with one another. Even though it is necessary to exercise one's imagination for this, this cannot mar the clarity of knowing that, though some room is left for imagination, no room is left for doubt.

MEDITATION — GUIDANCE

Meditation tools

Some tools can help us maintain our attention on the experiential level, so that our attention does not deviate to focus on stimuli, or thoughts, and be distracted from the experiential level.

When thoughts are running through our head and troubling our mind, our attention is not available to observe. Instead of thought serving us, thought controls us. This is like a horse riding a man – not how it is meant to be. Thought should be a tool we use for our benefit. All we need to do is take a step back, and instead of partaking in the activity, to observe it as a bystander. As a result of this observation, a disconnect is formed between the observer and thought, and there is no blind drive to think and develop each and every train of thought. So it is with sensations as well – the very observation of them releases us from their clutch.

The object we have chosen to observe during the meditation exercise, regardless of what it is, halts the ceaseless stream of thoughts, for thoughts are action and when observation begins, action stops. And then, once again, thought steals our attention for a moment, and once again we become aware of thinking, and then reconnect our attention to the experience, and the thread of thought is severed. We are no longer blindly dragged after the thought, but repeatedly become aware of the fact that our attention has drifted into the world of thoughts and daydreaming, and so we snap it back to reality, and to the experience that we are experiencing right now in this moment. This places us in the position of the external observer, no longer the operators of the action of thought, and when there is no one to think, thought gradually subsides.

Tagging thoughts at the initial stage

One of the techniques that can help us with the observation of thoughts is the tagging technique. If we want to establish awareness of thoughts, then every time thoughts arise, you need to try and tag each thought as soon as it arises. This is the first step in gaining familiarity with the contents of our thoughts. Tagging means we are becoming aware of the contents of our thoughts. When we tag, the tagger is no longer the one doing the thinking, and hence the thought dissipates, for there is no one to think it. With meditators who have yet to practice this for a sufficiently long period of time, a new thought emerges almost as soon as the previous one fades away. But have no fear – that is why we are here – to learn how to halt this uncontrollable stream of thoughts. Be patient, and with practice, success will come.

The types of tagging we are going to want to use are: "future," "past," "unnecessary," "anger," "unwanted," "concern." Oftentimes we will see that the most suitable tag for a thought is "nonsense." Many of the thoughts that arise are simply nonsense, and are not even entire thoughts, but simply fragments thereof. They have no meaning, and they arise simply because our mind does not wish to be still.

You can tag a thought by any name you wish. The first name that comes to mind is the correct one. Do not try to come up with the correct name, because that will restart a thought process. Use any name that comes to mind immediately – there is no need to complicate things. Notice how once a thought is tagged it fades away, for you are now the observer, not the thinker. Tagging is a very important lesson that must not be skipped, at least not in the initial stage of learning meditation. The importance of tagging stems from the fact that we think all day, and if we learn how to tag, we learn how to identify when the thought we are thinking is not healthy and harms our own wellbeing and that of others. If at that moment we know how to let this thought pass and remain in the experiential level without sinking into thoughts, if we learn that and that alone, we will already have made a great step forward to liberating stressors and mending our ways. Everything we do or say depends on our thought processes. Thus, if we become aware of our thoughts during meditation practice through tagging, and bring this awareness into our daily lives, when we run into harmful thoughts, negative thoughts, thoughts of anger and revulsion that harm us and others, even not during meditation, then we will not continue thinking these thoughts. It is clear that those who are not experienced in meditation will have many thoughts and will not be able to tag all of them. Nonetheless, try tagging as many as you can. How many you manage at first does not matter – over time, your rate of thinking will decline.

Paying attention to your breathing

A practiced meditator who wishes to keep his attention on the sensation of breathing, which is a highly effective meditational object, is recommended to keep his attention linked to the sensation of the entry and exit of air through his nostrils. If you are not an experienced meditator, you will need some tool to help you. It is recommended you use one of the techniques I will immediately detail. If one of these techniques does not work for you, try another. Certain techniques may suit some of the practitioners, whereas alternative techniques might suit others. Those who suffer from asthma, or a cold, or a problem in the sinuses, will find it difficult to observe the sensation of air going in and out of their nostrils and should instead direct their attention at other sites to that the air flows – the lungs as they fill up and empty, or the diaphragm as it rises and falls.

First technique – counting

The first technique to maintain observation of breathing is the counting technique – count your breaths silently, and thereby keep your attention connected to the experience of breathing. Count one during inhalation, one at exhalation, two at inhalation, two at exhalation and repeat... but do not count too high, ten is enough. Once you reach ten, begin counting back from one. This is a technique for people who love their numbers. Continue counting for a limited period of time, only until you notice that your thoughts are quiet. If you get the count wrong, do not try to recall the last number you counted – simply go back to counting from one.

Second technique – imagination

If numbers aren't you thing and you have a visual imagination, you can visualize breathing like a cloud, or like a wave in the sea, as you prefer. Imagine this wave shrinking as you inhale, and growing as you exhale. You can imagine this wave surrounded by a silver band. Imagine it however you like – the important thing is that it is sufficiently interesting to capture your attention, leaving you connected to your breathing.

Third technique – word

If you do not like numbers and your imagination is weak, you can use a word. For example – "peace." Say "peace" with every breath, or "peace" as you inhale and then again when you exhale. In any event, the word should be a positive one. The word accompanying the breathing adds interest, and thereby helps fix one's attention in place. It is not recommended you utter more than two words. You can, at first, say them out loud, but it is recommended you later speak them only in your mind.

One can also use a meaningless syllable or a series of

syllables generating a meaningless word. A meaningless word is even preferable, for meaning makes us start thinking. The meaning of a word is the understanding behind the sounds of speech, but the sound of a meaningless syllable is a clean experience of the sense of hearing.

I use a combination of three syllables that I speak in my inner speech in a single continuum:

Va He Va

That is, I express them internally as three separate syllables, but utter them in a single continuous sequence, as follows:

"Vaheva."

Techniques transmitted by the Piaseczno Rabbi

A letter written by one of Rabbi Kalonymus Kalman Shapira's students was presented in the book "Derech HaMelech" (*The Way of the King*). The student describes how the rabbi taught them techniques to silence their thoughts, and this is a summary of his description:

"As all know, the way of our teacher, as he reveals in his books, that the essence of a man (ego, desires) is what opposes divine inspiration, and should his mind and thoughts be stirred, then it will be very difficult for inspiration from above to be received. However, when man sleeps and his mind and thoughts are serene, then, precisely because he pays no mind to himself, can inspiration from above come... while man sleeps, he cannot want anything, for he is asleep. Therefore, the idea is that one will bring himself to a sleep-like state even though he is awake, and his desires are active. That is, by silencing the thoughts and desires constantly roiling through one's mind – for such is the way of thoughts: they get tangled up with one another – it can be difficult to draw away from them... and then our teacher provided genuine advice on how to silence one's thoughts... and spoke then that the person should begin to observe his thoughts for a brief time, a few moments, asking himself: 'What do I think?' And then he will slowly feel his head emptying and his thoughts end their usual frenzy... one can use the observation of a clock, the little hand that barely moves over time, as a tool to soothe desires and thoughts. After the silencing, meant to bring some inspiration from above, our teacher instructed us to say the verse, 'God teach me your ways' (Psalms 86:11) in the special melody conceived by our teacher."

The student then cites the words of the rabbi on how silencing brings about a mending of our ways:

"And he said then that the silence can be used for the mending of all bad ways, but not negatively, only positively, by reversing the bad tendency. Thus, one suffering from laziness, will be focused not on eliminating laziness, but on cultivating diligence. He explained this that one can see this in a crying baby, the more one tells him not to cry! Speaking to him will merely make him cry even more."

It is of course clear that meditation can result in a mending of one's ways. A person who is capable of cleansing himself of stress does not tend to anger, and his conduct becomes more moderate. But what is the source of inspiration we acquire via meditation? Who actually provides us with these insights? Who are those who aid us and seemingly whisper to us ideas and solutions to our problems?

According to ancient sources, meditation opens us up to the source of ultimate wisdom, to a parallel universe that is spiritual in nature, with spiritual entities that can help man with advice and knowledge, should they choose to do so, enabling man to suddenly know whatever he needs to know in order to succeed.

Those who knew the names of these entities could initiate contact with them by calling out their name. Some of the "meaningless" words used by the ancients during meditation were actually the names of spiritual entities they called on for heavenly assistance, primarily in the form of inspiration. Hence, the word you recite while meditating – beyond being a tool helping you to maintain attention from distraction – also draws to you a spiritual influence that match the frequency of the syllables you are expressing in your heart, and you should keep this in mind when you choose which word to use. Something with a pure and good source should be chosen.

The sounds of the syllables are the experiential portion of letters, whereas the deciphering of their meaning is an action, not an experience, and requires concentration, leading to a loss of awareness. For example: a man might listen to an orchestra and enjoy the sounds of all instruments playing in harmony. The various instruments do not interfere with one another – rather it is the harmony between them that generates a greater whole.

In contrast, when a man is in a room packed with people talking with one another, he must zero in on a single conversation, because when one encodes the meaning of the sounds of speech, and not merely experiences them, one exercises the thought, and the action of thought, like any other action, requires concentration, and concentration results in distraction.

According to ancient sources, the spiritual activity of the ancient kabbalists of Israel was primarily to listen to the sound of various letter combinations without trying to interpret them. They would deal with the dissolution and reconstitution of letter combinations without trying to interpret them.

In the book "Shaarei Tzedek" (Gates of Righteousness) written by the kabbalist Rabbi Shem Tov Sepharadi (some attribute the book to Rabbi Abraham Abulafia), the Rabbi Shem Tov recounts how he met a mystic teacher who taught him kabbalah: "... and he taught me through the combination and transformations and gematria and the other ways of the Book of Yetzirah, and in every path he would let me walk it for two weeks until the form was etched deep upon my heart , and so he continued for four months (in which new and useful ideas would arise out of the combinations and the gematria) and would command me to erase everything, and would tell me: 'son, it is not the intent for you to fixate on any limited form, and even though this form is the most refined of all, for this is the way of the names, **the more that they are indecipherable to you, that is their virtue for themselves,** until you reach the act of the power that is not your own, but that of the divine working through you.' I replied as follows: 'And why do you write books that include both philosophy and meaningless combinations of letters?' And he told me: 'For you and those like you, who love philosophy, to attract their rational mind according to their nature, so that this might lead them to the knowledge of the holy names.' And he took out for me books composed from letters, names and gematrias, which one could never make any sense of, for they are not composed of meaningful letter combinations, and he told me: 'This is the way of the names!' And truly, I did not wish to see it, for my mind could not accept it..." (chapter 10, page 21).

If indeed the composer of the book "Shaarei Tzedek" (Gates of Righteousness) is Rabbi Abraham Abulafia, then this book was written around 750 years ago. Rabbi Abraham Abulafia lived between 1240-1291. This was a period during the waning of the Golden Age of the Jews in Spain, in which many Jews were engaged in philosophy and this teacher of mysticism wished to emphasize to his students the importance of letter combinatorics, and to bring the practice closer to their rational mind, which is why he incorporated into the books he wrote philosophical arguments as well, to explain the "way of names" as he called it. However, the truth is that **"the more that they are indecipherable to you, that is their virtue,"** for the purpose of the letter combinatorics is to bring man to a state of the detachment from the body – **"until you reach the act of power that is not in your possession but your mind and thought are in his possession,"** that is, until your soul dominates thought without any resistance, and is reflected in thought as in a clean mirror.

It is written in the book Sulam Ha'Aliah (Ladder of

Ascent), chapter 10, page 75: "And know that by reciting the letters and mixing them, these great things will be achieved, for they are the source of all wisdom and knowledge (Letters and numbers are 32 physical containers that store information, and thus are actually a threshold between spirit and matter – between heaven and earth: they are the psychophysical connection), and they themselves are the mater of prophecy and are reflected in the mirror of prophecy as if they are thick bodies who take shape and speak to a person face to face by the power of imagination inherent in his mind's eye. And this hidden power embedded in the letters is rejected by the rational mind at first glance, but if one seeks to delve deeper with a pure mind, he will know that these are the angels, and they are those who tutor the prophet through the mirror of prophecy, wisdom and knowledge that there is no doubt of. And this is clear and known to those who possess true knowledge. For with the power of letters, all living beings were created, as is written in the Book of Yetzirah – "3 main letters, 7 double letters, 12 simple letters," and this is a true thing and there is no doubt about it at all."[1]

---

1. Rabbi Shem Tov Sepharadi is relying here on the Jewish practice of *gematria* – assigning a numerical value to letters and creating new words by recombining numerical and letter values into new forms, until the ultimate source of knowledge embodied in the letters, reveals itself. As Rabbi Avraham Abulafia says explicitly in one of his books: "When you roll the name over and over again, eventually the name itself reveals its secret to you."

META-COGNITION

The Exception Requiring Explanation

Is it possible to discern between fact and fiction? When I say fiction, I am referring to anything that is not real, be it a deliberate lie, a misidentification, or an illusion an individual genuinely believes in. I seek a given characteristic that can be used to distinguish between an objective fact and a subjective lie.

A clear distinction between fact and fiction is that fiction is an invention – the fruit of imagination, whether deliberate or otherwise, and hence the chance that two separate minds would come up with the same fiction without pre-coordination is very slim. Should a correlation be found between two sources of information that could not have been coordinated, and should this correlation occur at a high level of detail, this correlation is evidence of the information arriving from both sources being fact, not fiction. A high level of coordination between two sources is not plausible unless both experienced the same events they recounted, and that is what makes their versions match.

Actually, it is not only improbable for such correlation

to be generated by chance, it is impossible! Statistical variations allowing for such fluke correlations to occur, become increasingly improbable the larger the sample size is, and beyond a certain sample size, the statistical norm becomes essentially a natural law.

Imagination is wild and creative

The human imagination is wild; its creativity cannot be predicted, and hence a precise correlation between two human minds, each separately creating an identical story through its unique power of imagination is flat-out impossible.

In fact, any inner process taking place in a closed system cannot generate precise correlation with the external world. If correlation exists, it is a deviation that can only be explained by an external reason that exists outside the system and influences it from the outside; there must be some hidden communication of the system with the outside world, which means that though we think the system is closed, this is not truly the case.

Evidence without context

Physical evidence is a deviation from the norm; a break from the natural and the usual by an external disturbance. The deviation indicates an external factor interfering with the regular activity of the system, even if we do not know what it is. Whether the deviation has an explanation or not, the deviation itself is evidence. However, absent explanation, it is evidence without context. Even if we cannot provide an explanation for it, we cannot ignore the deviation as if it were no more than a random, insignificant malfunction. One cannot remain indifferent in face of the deviation. The exception is what is unexpected, and that is precisely why it requires an explanation. The exception is not subject to the laws according to which the system operates, for it shatters them, and hence it must emerge from outside the system.

All comes from dust and returns to dust – even the sun fades away

All we create in matter ceases to exist over time. Any form imprinted in matter must one day crumble into dust. As King Solomon has said: "All go to the same place; all come from dust, and to dust all return." (Ecclesiastes 3:20). If we invest time and effort to shape matter into form, it is like unto building a castle in the sand. It rapidly decays, and soon will have no longer exist. The stronger the material is, the longer its existence lasts. But one way or the other, the fate of everything created from matter is to crumble back to earth.

Even the sun fades away. All that is matter must crumble away in time, fade away, break down and scatter.

The requisite question is: Since destruction is natural and ongoing, what makes discrete, material bodies form in the first place? Why is the universe not composed of a uniform sludge of material homogenously filling all space? In other words, if chaos is the natural state of affairs, and that is where everything flows and that is the balanced state in which particles of matter reach serenity and equality, then how are order and form generated to begin with?

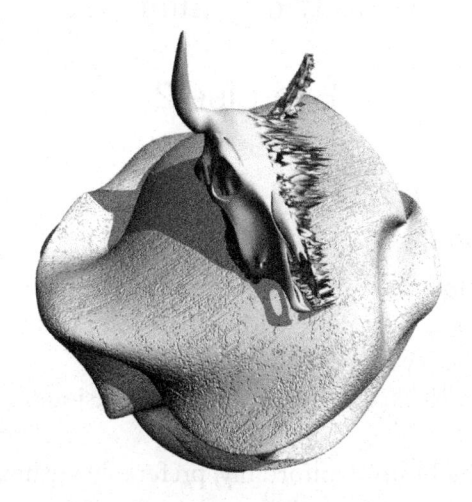

All come from dust, and to dust all return

Stop reading the manual now, and we will meet again this evening when it comes time for Exercise 2.

MEDITATION – GUIDANCE

Exercise 2

Instructions
It is time for the evening exercise of the first day.
- Look for a quiet place with a chair you can sit on comfortably.
- Place a clock nearby so you can occasionally glance at it.
- Sit straight up, comfortably, preferably without leaning backwards.
- The head should be straight up and comfortable.
- We will start with a few minutes of sitting without doing anything.

Out of the resulting silence, begin listening to your sensations. These sensations are transmitted to our mind through the nervous system. The neural stimuli of pleasure and pain make us respond, by thought or by action, and this results in distraction.

Observation of the sensations generates a realization in us that the sensations are foreign to us, and enables us to detach from them, not to be identified with our body, who feels them. These are electrical stimuli passing through the nervous system, no more. This is a part of the body's technical mechanism that is not part of our selfhood.

Ending our pursuit after pleasure and escape from pain generates inner quiet from which a more sublime satisfaction is revealed – a permanent inner joy, which is independent on external stimuli of pleasure, and is not troubled by any external stimuli of pain.

The sensations are the primary factor resulting in focusing one's attention and are the root of distraction, and hence I view the observation of these sensations as the ultimate meditation object. The dependence on sensations is the foundational point from which one must be liberated to achieve awareness. Even if the purpose of meditation is to reach a higher spiritual level of awareness, this purpose will never be achieved unless we first shed our identification with the body, mostly generated from yearning for the sensations of pleasure, and the fear of pain. Listening to these sensations generates detachment from them, but only if you observe them as an outside observer who does not judge but only observes things as they are.

Any observation, regardless of what, halts our activity, whether that of the body or of the mind, because observation and action cannot coexist – one stops the other. Since activity stops, awareness begins. But observation of sensations results in more than stopping the activity. It also uproots the cause of activity from its foundation, for such observation dissociates the observer from the stimuli of sensations – pleasure and pain – which are the motivation for actions. Observing sensations not only blocks the activity, it halts what generated the activity to begin with; that is, it pushes away the stimuli that had triggered the activity to begin with.

Some observe the sensations of the entire body – scanning the body from head to foot and back again. With me, observing the sensation of breathing had the strongest impact, and that is what I recommend.

We will quietly listen to the sensations generated in the act of breathing, and we will now add to it the word we have chosen. I usually breathe and think the word while I exhale. Everything needs to be done without exerting yourself. Exertion is a sign of struggle – a desire to achieve something by force. In meditation, things need to happen on their own, through natural flow, out of acceptance of what is, be it good or bad.

- Meditate for about 20 minutes.
- At the end of the exercise, do not open your eyes immediately. Remain seated for a few minutes in order to gradually return to you usual state of consciousness.

Meditation brings absolute acceptance of reality as it is here and now, without any judgement of it, and without any desire to change it. This is an expression of absolute trust in divine providence, and complete abolition of private desire, which derives from the ego, until it does not matter in the least what happens. Should one eventuality come to pass, it is certainly for the best, and should another pass, that too is for the best. This is not a philosophy that claims all is for the best. This is an experience you undergo when you reach a place far beyond good and evil, for when pursuit of pleasure and flight from pain ends, individual will ends, and the universal will embodied in reality is revealed. This leads you to become part of something that is bigger than you, and opens you up to receive all the goodness and wisdom existence seeks to provide you with.

Then, without intending to, the actions you perform will express this higher will, and the thoughts you think will come from this higher source.

Many people believe there is a creator, and that all that happens in the world comes from him and him alone, but not many people have full trust in the creator doing the best thing possible – that is the hard part! In practice, one sees many wrongdoings in the world, until it seems there is no justice in the world, and it is very hard to accept that all is for the best. And indeed, there is no justification to think this, if it is merely a thought. But if this is the experience you have, when during meditation you transcend good and evil, and become aware that the root of good and evil is one, after such an experience, there is no more room for any thought.

There is a portal through which one can arrive at this absolute certainty, a path that leads back to paradise. This portal is called meditation, and it brings man to the quality of equanimity, that is: to be accepting of all that occurs, not due to indifference, but due to knowledge that behind all conflicts reality seemingly portrays, there is harmony, and this harmony reveals itself only to those who observe reality without judgement, which is what happens naturally when thought is quieted, for the source of judgement is in thought, since judgment is just a form of thought, thus if thought is abolished, there can be no judgment.

- Faith is acknowledging that all comes from above.
- Trust is recognizing that all is for the best.

One cannot arrive at this level of trust without first achieving faith, but he who acquires for himself the capacity of faith and has not also acquired trust, is an unfortunate man indeed. On the one hand, he knows that there is a divine providence guiding all events, but on the other hand he sees a world filled with injustice – the seeming contradiction may well lead him to hate the ruler of the world. It therefore follows that in this sense faith without trust is worse than a total lack of faith.

The awareness one reaches via meditation is a direct experience of existence, without any buffers between the self and reality, not even the mediation of one's own critical thinking. As soon as you begin relying on a mediator, you are displaying alienation to reality, for you have thereby proven you do not really want to know it firsthand – you apparently are not interested in facts, but in stories.

A mediator does not generate a connection – rather, it generates separation and a barrier. For example: we have gotten used to relying on the opinion of experts, allowing them to mediate between ourselves and reality, instead of exploring it ourselves. An expert should share his knowledge with us, he needs to enlighten us. Not lead us like blind men. One should not trust others where it is possible to clarify the truth – after all, even the greatest expert may err, perhaps even lie for his own benefit. What reason is there, therefore, to prioritize trust over first-hand knowledge?

Words are not evidence of anything, even if they were written millennia ago, because errors and lies have also existed for millennia

You should learn from every individual the knowledge they are prepared to share, but trust no one. Trust weakens you; knowledge strengthens you. The things you accept should have weight in and of themselves, not just because of who you heard them from; they should be insights, not just words of authority.

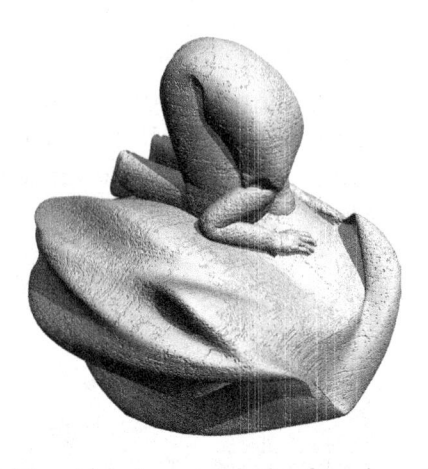

Naïve faith, which does not derive from investigation, but from fear of questioning and doubting, leads to burying one's head in the sand, and to a cult of personality

The only way an individual can maintain his childlike innocence is by refusing to open his eyes and observing reality as it is, insisting instead to see things as he would like them to be – this is an illusion, however sweet it may be.

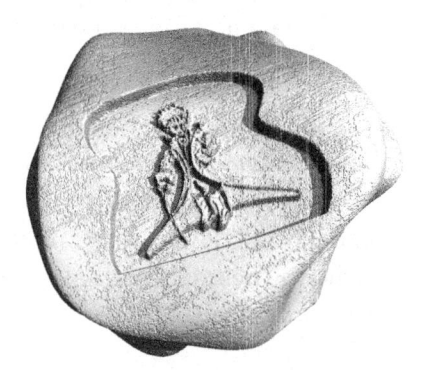

The book *The Little Prince* expresses a yearning for childhood innocence

The motif of concealing reality as it can be seen, in order to preserve your inner innocence (the lamb), appears as a central motif in the book The Little Prince, and it is also a central motif in Christianity, which sees in the innocence of children, who question nothing, the pinnacle of faith. The ancient priesthoods of Egypt venerated the lamb as a symbol of innocence, which they also highly valued. The Sabbatian Movement, which arose from belief in Shabtai Tzvi being the Messiah, also pushed the idea of innocent faith under the guise of Judaism.

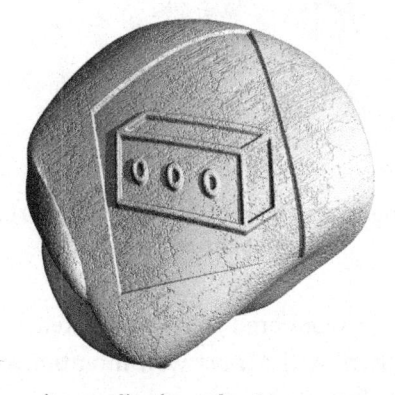

Obscuring reality in order to preserve your innocence (the lamb hidden in the box) is a central motif in the book *The Little Prince*

The innocent lamb walks unaware to a single terminal location – the slaughterhouse. The people who believe in words, instead of striving to achieve direct, unmediated contact with reality, are in fact the root of all evil in the world, for because of them, the world is ruled over by ravenous wolves and we all suffer. The sheep are those who empower the wolf to rule over us all. The wolf is ravenous by nature, it cannot change. But the sheep empowers him by choice – at any point they can choose to open their eyes, but they prefer the sweet, familiar illusion they wish to believe.

**Sheep are the root of evil in the world,
not the wolves**

Have you ever wondered why any system of rules and values – created by the most well-intentioned men, who wish nothing but to govern a righteous and just society – never worked? How come a small elite who unjustly lord over everyone else by force is always formed? Why is this?

The conceivers of communism meant to promote social justice and equality. What does communism proclaim? From each according to their ability, to each according to their need! The conceivers of capitalism also intended to provide a just equality of opportunity to everyone to build themselves up and succeed in accordance with their actions. Moderate socialism, whose basis is the taxing of the rich to support a welfare system for all, worked well enough in the West in the post-World War Two era. How then did violent criminals take over communism and eventually, as of today, capitalism as well? There is now no fair competition in the markets of the countries espousing capitalism, only monopolistic mega corporations ruled over by a tiny circle of magnates. Why does this repeatedly occur that good laws, legislated with the best of intentions, eventually become tools of evil and corruption?

That is what happens when you separate law from justice. Law must be subordinated to justice. If you accept the idea that the letter of the law is above the spirit of the law, instead of the converse, then we have already consented to the idea that law supersedes justice, or at least is valid in and of its own, independently of justice.

How did John D. Rockefeller and his business partners gain control over ninety percent of the oil industry in the United States at the time, despite all the antitrust laws meant to prevent the emergence of such monopolies? His lawyers found loopholes in the letter of the law that allowed him to act against the spirit of the law! If the judges had prioritized the spirit of the law over the letter of the law, this would not have happened. But the judges and the public were sold a lie that the letter of the law outweighed the spirit of the law. Hence, the justice system was twisted to serve the criminals, instead of serving the public by condemning them. And nonetheless, the public trusts the authorities blindly.

The letter of the law and the spirit of the law are two possible ways to regard rules, or laws. To obey the letter of the law is to follow the literal reading of the words of the law, whereas following the spirit of the law is to follow the purpose for which the law was written. Although it is usual to follow both the letter and the spirit, the two are commonly referenced when they are in opposition – that is when we have to make a choice between the two, and if the wrong choice is made, the legal system is corrupted, And from there the rot spreads to all other places, and as the saying goes: the rot starts at the top. King Solomon said: "Furthermore, I have seen under the sun that in the place of justice, there is wickedness and in the place of righteousness, there is wickedness." (Ecclesiastes 3:16)

As soon as we consented to a separation of powers, we freed the judicial authority from the legislative authority, and separated law from justice. As soon as we agreed to make legislators obligated to the constitution, we subordinated justice to law.

Justice, justice, you shall pursue

"You shall appoint judges and officers in all your gates, which the LORD your God gives you, according to your tribes, and they shall judge the people with just judgment." (Deuteronomy 16:18) Why does the Bible need to stress that judgement will be just? After all, judgement is meant to let the judge hear the arguments of contending parties and determine which of them is just. It is therefore clear that law must be just and judgment fair.

Yet those familiar with secular justice systems know how complicated this issue actually is. Law is not necessarily justice, and justice is not necessarily law. The oath a lawyer swears upon taking office in Israel's civil court, is to assist the court in upholding the law – law, not justice. In an interview, the Dean of the Faculty of Law in Tel-Aviv University recounted how he always warns students on his first lecture upon the start of the academic year that they are in the university to study law, not justice. In one case, a judge in an Israeli court told the plaintiff – "I agree with you, you are right, but the law is against you!" Charles Dickens was the first to say "the law is an ass" in Oliver Twist. That's "ass" as in stubborn, stupid donkey, not the American word for what you sit on. Since Dickens' day, many folk have had good reason to agree. Meaning the law is what is written in it, and what is not, is not law. It is therefore clear that law and justice are entirely different things, and one can certainly separate them from each other. (See an expanded discussion on this matter in appendix C.)

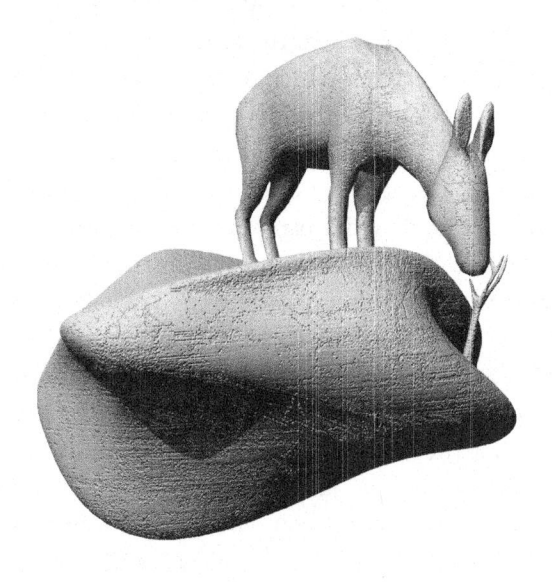

The law is a stubborn, stupid donkey

Post-Exercise 2 Report

Take advantage of this moment, when you are right after the exercise, and the experience is completely fresh, to fill in the post-exercise report.

Report for exercise 2	Date and time:
Possible influence	Mark with checkmark
I felt calm	
The pace of my thoughts slowed down	
There were moments in which I had no thoughts at all	
I felt emotional discomfort	
I felt physical discomfort	
I felt stress relief	
I experienced involuntary movements	
Old memories were stirred	
I felt like smiling	
I felt inner peace	
At the end, I felt refreshed	

META-COGNITION

Seeing is believing

We have earlier said that man must seek direct contact with reality rather than look for mediators that will stand between him and the direct experience. Or as the saying goes: "seeing is believing" – it is better to see with your own eyes than hear stories told by others who have seen. Nonetheless, appearances can be deceptive. Therefore, one cannot rely only on the eyesight of one man, not even yourself, so you must cross-reference information from two or more sources.

A judge who has seen with his own eyes the act he is discussing also requires witnesses in order to clarify the facts, and cannot rely solely on his sight. The judge is an expert in rendering judgement, but his testimony has no precedence over that of any other eyewitness. Hence, even if the judge has witnessed the case he is presiding over with his own eyes, he must seek out another witness to cross reference and validate the information, because even a judge might make identification mistakes.

Therefore, a judge presiding alone cannot rely on his own eyewitness, but if several judges are presiding, and two of them have witnessed the deed, it is possible to investigate and cross-reference the information, making it possible to rely on the testimony of the judges who have seen the case with their own eyes, after they are investigated by the other presiding judges. The exception is cases of a severe crime, in which the witness develops anger towards the defendant, and finds it difficult to judge him justly, in which case he cannot serve as a judge in any event. So says the Talmud.

MEDITATION — GUIDANCE

Exercise 3

Instructions
Good morning, it is now time for the morning exercise of the second day:
- Look for a quiet place, with a chair on which you can sit comfortably.
- Sit straight up comfortably, best without leaning backwards. The head must be held up straight comfortably. If during deep meditation your head droops, never mind, go with the flow.
- A clock must be placed nearby.
- The duration of the exercise is 20 minutes.
- Start with a few minutes of sitting without doing anything.
- Feel yourself breathing.
- Say the word in your heart with every breath you take.
- Let things happen. Whatever needs to happen will happen. We will let things happen without trying to change them.

Some people suffer from great lack of sleep, for their lives have a hectic pace. For them, meditation is a deep rest. Others constantly worry, and to them meditation will bring inner peace. Not right away perhaps, but with time. Everyone and the place where he is, from there they ascend to a better place. Those deep in the earth have a longer way to go until they reach the heavens – until they achieve complete serenity. There are also those who merit a vision and inspiration, answers to questions that have been troubling them. These are different stages on the same ladder, with its feet in the ground, and its head in the heavens.

- Glance at the clock occasionally.
- If it is time to end the exercise, do not open your eyes immediately. Stay quiet for a few minutes and open your eyes gradually so as not to shock your nervous system.

Post-Exercise 3 Report

As soon as you complete the exercise, while the experience is still fresh, fill out the post-exercise report.

Report for exercise 3	Date and time:
Possible influence	Mark with checkmark
I felt calm	
The pace of my thoughts slowed down	
There were moments in which I had no thoughts at all	
I felt emotional discomfort	
I felt physical discomfort	
I felt stress relief	
I experienced involuntary movements	
Old memories were stirred	
I felt like smiling	
I felt inner peace	
At the end, I felt refreshed	

META-COGNITION

What is a presumption?

What is a presumption and what is the difference between it and evidence?

A presumption is not an investigation of the truth. When we presume a man to be innocent, that does not mean he is truly innocent – just that until proven otherwise, he enjoys the benefit of the doubt, and the burden of proof is on those claiming otherwise.

Since a presumption does not clarify the doubt, it may be that two presumptions will contradict each other, and despite that, both will be accepted as temporary truths, until it is proven otherwise. For example, a man who had two servants living in his house and preparing his food, and he was poisoned by one of them. We know the man was poisoned by a meal prepared solely by his two servants and that they alone had access to the food he ate in the meal where he was poisoned, and that the ingredients they both used to prepare the meal were found to contain no poison. Each servant claims the other explicitly told him that he planned to poison his employer due to his hatred of him, and asked his colleague to join in the conspiracy, but was turned down.

In such a case, even though it is clear to us that one of the two servants must have poisoned his employer, for there is no alternative possibility, we will still presume the innocence of both, since there is no evidence indicating which poisoned the man, or whether both did, colluding with one another. Hence, we presume the innocence of both, acquitting both. This is a complete exoneration, and they will be presumed innocent in every way, without a shadow of a doubt, until we find out otherwise, even though the acquittal is solely on the basis of reasonable doubt.

A presumption is a determination made before evidence is found to clarify doubt, because even prior to the discovery of the truth, during the uncertainty, you need to decide what to do until the truth comes to light. Therefore, although it is not possible for both servants to be innocent, if we acquit one, logic dictates we should condemn the other. There is no contradiction since the presumption does not clarify the truth, only tells us what to do until the truth comes to light.

Evidence is not like that – it is not possible to prove both something and its exact opposite. If this happened, then there is clearly an error in the evidence somewhere.

To summarize: the presumption of one entity does not aid or hinder another entity, for a presumption does not clarify the truth, and hence each entity is judged on its own merits, and a presumption held for one entity need not be compatible with a presumption held by another entity.

A presumption answers one question and one question only: what to do here and now. It has no answers in regard to the past or in regards to the future, because questions such as "what was?" or "what will be?" are questions relating to what occurred or will occur in reality, and a presumption only answers the question of what to do now, in the present, until reality is clarified.

Two entities as a single subject of inquiry

We have already shown there is a direct connection between meditation and the awareness of thought processes. Being aware of your thought processes is important because we don't want to follow destructive trains of thought. This is how we make our mind healthy. That is the reason I constantly bring up meta-cognitive insights, taken from all kinds of sources. Here are some insights I picked from the Talmud, which show us the Talmudic way of thinking in states of uncertainty as part of covering the issue of meta-cognition.

The Talmud relates to cases in which several subjects of inquiry are deliberated on as a single subject. In such a case, each subject of inquiry is not decided on its own account, as we saw in the previous case of the servants poisoning their master, but a single presumption governs all of them together.

One way in which a single decision is valid to several subjects in doubt, is in the case where both questions concerning the two subjects are dependent on one another. Hence, the conclusion of one question determines the other question as well. That is why in such a case you only discuss a single question – the question under discussion that is at the pinnacle of the pyramid of questions, and the question concerning the primary subject is determined according to the presumption that is relevant to it. Any conclusion or sentencing reached upon the primary subject, also applies to the other subjects that depend on it, even if they have contradictory presumptions.

For example: A man borrowed money from his friend. The time came to repay. The lender claimed he wasn't paid. The borrower is not denying he took the loan, but he claims he has already repaid his debt. If there is any evidence concerning the loan, but no evidence concerning the repayment, then the borrower remains a debtor until proven otherwise.

But then the man dies before he repays his debt, and his son inherits him. Though the son never borrowed anything, and his father was obligated to repay his debt only on account of presumption, the presumption of liability to pay the debt is inherited by the son along with his father's assets, so the question of whether the son must pay depends on whether the father must pay. The son comes on behalf of the father, and hence the deliberation is not reopened in regard to the son separately, and although the presumption for one subject is of no benefit to another, in cases where questions depend upon one another, determining the question at the top of the hierarchy of questions settles all of the questions dependent on it.

But all this only applies if the lender demanded his debt from the father while he was still alive. If the time for repayment came after the father has already passed away, and the lender came to demand repayment directly from the son, then the son is exempted from repayment of the debt since the father is not present to present his case to the judge, and only the son is the subject of deliberation. As there is no presumption of liability for debt on the son, for it is not he who borrowed the money, and the debt is not certain since the father may have already repaid the debt but failed to pass on the receipt to his heir, reasonable doubt requires us not to charge the son for that which he has no presumption of obligation for.

• • •

A second case in which several entities are deliberated under a single question is one where the two entities are intermixed and there is no discernible difference between them. Then they become a group, and a single doubt applies to them all. Such group doubt is determined according to the presumption applicable to most subjects in the group.

For instance: many infants are born in the same hospital, and since they are not yet known to their parents, and look more or less the same, it is not possible to distinguish between them. On the cradle of each baby, his family name is written in order to avoid switching between them. But what if the nurse caring for them should make a mistake and place each in the cradle of the other? The only thing that could distinguish between the infants were their cradles, on which their names were written. Thus, it is only their placement that enabled identification, for there is no distinguishing mark on the babies themselves. It therefore follows that from the moment the nurse removed the baby from his crib, to bring him to his mother, he lost his identity, for it is no longer possible to tell who he is. This means that the separation between the entity and its distinctive mark is what generated the doubt in this case. But this did not transform the doubt into one over the entire group. What would make the doubt spread to the entire group is if the children intermixed with one another, that is – left their permanent location in the crib. It is this mix-up that united them as a group. In such a case, doubt about a group applies to all the intermixed babies. And since they are all discussed as a group, one may assume that each of the babies belong to the majority. For example: if most children are born to parents who are citizens of the state, and by law children to parents who are citizens of the state also receive citizenship, then doubt requires us to provide all babies with citizenship because we settle this general doubt according to the presumption applicable to most babies, even if some of them were born to non-citizens. This is the most reasonable and correct determination in this case, even if it is not the truth, for a presumption is never "the truth" in the factual sense, but a reasonable working assumption, which should be assumed so long as it is not known otherwise.

What if all the other children are sleeping in their cribs, and when the attending nurse comes to return one of the babies to his crib, she cannot remember what crib she took him from, but there is only one cradle available? In such a case there is no doubt, because there is only one baby under discussion, and one free cradle.

The problem begins if there is more than one baby who has been separated from his crib and removed from his fixed location. Only then does the separation generate a mix-up.

What if the attending nurse placed a baby in the crib of another baby, without noticing that there is already another baby in this crib?

In this case, one of the babies that is in the crib is in the wrong crib, whereas the other baby, which was there before, has not been put in the wrong crib, having remained there – only we don't know who he is, making the doubt concerning his identity separate.

What if all the labels that were on the cribs on which the babies are placed all fell off? In such a case, the doubt is applicable to each and every baby in and of itself, since none of them were removed from their fixed place, which means there is no mix-up to render them a group. Even though we have doubt about the identity of all the babies, that doubt applies to each baby separately. Doubt about a group is a doubt that derives from the mix-up of the subjects, so that if there had been no mix-up, we would have no doubt. If even without the mix-up there is doubt, this is not doubt about a group, and you do not discuss them all together, but each entity constitutes a separate subject of discussion in and of itself.

Only a doubt about a group is determined according to the majority. It is the mix-up that connects the individuals and generates the majority. But if each stands separately, in their fixed location, even if we do not know who he is, because his mark has been lost, there is no connection here between the doubts, but a separate doubt for each baby, and their presumptions do not join together to generate a majority determination.

All these are the rules in determining doubts according to a presumption as they are outlined in the Talmud.

By the way, insofar as babies are concerned, there is no need to be overly concerned your baby might be switched, for the hospitals found a solution – a label tied to the baby's hand, on which his family name is clearly marked. So there is no need to worry when giving birth in a hospital regarding this problem, a problem that has been of great concern to women in the past, who were weary of making the change from giving birth at home with the aid of a trusted midwife to giving birth in a more sterile and professional, but less personal, hospital.

To summarize: in some conditions, there are several entities where the same doubt applies to all. In such a case, a single decision is valid for all. I call such a situation a "sharing of doubts." There is sharing on the basis of hierarchy, and there is sharing on the basis of common grouping, as explained above.

In my opinion, the Talmud should be titled the masterpiece of meta-cognition, since it teaches its student to think correctly. Correct thought is a skill that forms the basis for all wisdom. In other words, it teaches us to research correctly, so the research leads to factually correct findings.

Some believe that the extraordinary mental power of the Jewish people derives from the study of the Talmud. Universities are not unique to the Jewish People and hence cannot be held responsible for this success. In South Korea, many are convinced that it is study of the Talmud that makes the Jewish People wise, and many homes possess a Korean translation of the Talmud. Well, it is not exactly the full Talmud. It is rather a book containing a collection of tracts from the Talmud, mostly the tales of the Jewish sages.

"We were very curious about the high academic achievements of the Jews," said Yang-Sam-Ma, South Korean ambassador to Israel between 2008-2011, in an interview to the program "Tarbut HaYom" (Culture Today). "Jews have a very high rate of Nobel Prize laureates in all fields: literature, sciences and economics. This is an incredible achievement. We tried to understand the secret of the Jewish People – how do they, more than other nations, manage such impressive achievements? What makes Jews so smart? The conclusion we reached is that one of your secrets is the study of the Talmud.

"Jews study the Talmud from a young age, and that helps them, in our opinion, to develop extraordinary capabilities. This understanding led us to conclude that we should also teach our children the Talmud. We believe that if we teach our children the Talmud, we too can be geniuses. That is what is behind our decision to bring this book into almost every home in South Korea."

Who knows, Maybe they are right? Even though not all Jews learn Talmud, perhaps those who do learn it have some kind of a subtle influence on the nation as a whole.

MEDITATION — GUIDANCE

Exercise 4

Instructions

It is time for the evening exercise of the second day:
- Look for a quiet place with a chair you can sit on comfortably.
- Sit straight up, comfortably, preferably without leaning backwards.
- The head should be straight up and comfortable.
- Be sure to keep a clock somewhere nearby.
- The length of the exercise is 20 minutes.
- Start with a few minutes of sitting without doing anything.
- Then begin feeling your breathing.
- After a while, begin repeating the word in your inner speech with every breath.

• • •

It is time to meet our inner enemy – the force that operates us when we are distracted. What is this force that operates us when we work automatically and without paying any attention?

This force is the subconscious.

A few examples:

- A man scratches his forehead when he is sound asleep. Who does this action when there is no one home? The subconscious!
- A man drives home every day and is so used to the route he can drive it on autopilot. That is exactly what he does, and at the end of the trip he wakes up, as if from a dream, after wandering in his mind, in other worlds he remembers nothing from his drive home. Who then drove the car? Who navigated it all the way with no one home? The subconscious!
- A person is speaking on the phone and at the same time running to catch the bus. The person's attention is directed at the phone call – so who is making sure he does not fall over while running? The subconscious!

There are two situations in which the subconscious takes action and assumes command, leading us to operate on autopilot:

1. When our attention is captivated by a new and fascinating thing, and thereby distracted from our main activity.
2. When we are engaged in a repetitive action, and out of boredom our attention wanders elsewhere, because attention always seeks out the new and interesting.

In fact, both of these situations are one and the same. Our attention focuses on a single thing, and thus it is distracted from another thing. One may well say that it is the focus that generates the distraction. It seems to us that being focused is the opposite of being distracted, but that is not the case. It is indeed the focus that generates distraction. If we are focused on only one thing, we are in any event distracted from the other things. Awareness is a state where attention is not focused on anything, and hence is not distracted by anything. Awareness is a state where we choose not to be focused on anything, and do not prefer anything over anything else, but accept everything. As soon as we express our self-desires by preferring one thing over the other, and focus our attention on it, a distraction from the thing we do not desire immediately forms, and every distraction grants the subconscious a chance to rule. The subconscious holds our Achilles heel, where we stumble into the net of those who seek to rule over us. Above all else, you must be mindful of the activity of your thoughts, for it is the source of every action.

Our attention is always directed outwards, to the external stimuli, and so it is distracted from what is going on inside us. If you take time out and direct your attention inwards, to your inner experiences – your sensations and thoughts and emotions, and especially your thoughts – you will discover that thought does not rest for even a single second. A continuous stream of thoughts constantly runs through your mind. Who authorized this activity? Who gave it permission? If the brain is likened to a computer, it should serve us when we need it. How dare the servant take over its master and assume command, and incessantly think, when we have no need of this? Nor is it difficult to halt the bustle of thought. What is harder is being aware that thoughts are scurrying within us, for our attention is used to focus on the world outside, distracting us from what occurs within.

The way to draw our attention back within is through practicing meditation. "Practicing" is not quite the right word, for it implies action, and in meditation you are supposed to avoid action, for it is harder to notice the background grinding of the subconscious while you are engaged in activity. As soon as you decide to halt any initiated action of your own, however, you will suddenly discover that still, the activity does not cease, for there are external forces working on you. This is how you become aware of your hidden companion – your subconscious. You become aware that this hidden companion has his own agenda, and undermines you, and its activity must be halted – that is what the practice of meditation does.

Our attention usually tends to focus on what is happening outside – on the external stimuli – and hence meditation is usually perceived as internal observation: the objects of meditation usually tend to direct attention to our inner world. It is true that during meditation, we wish to draw our attention towards the inner experiences, from which we are usually distracted, but not at the cost of external experiences, because doing so would once again result in focusing on one thing while distracting ourselves from another. In meditation, we want to open ourselves up in all directions – to be aware of both what is happening inside us and what is happening outside of us – to be fully aware with no distractions. All that remains outside the consciousness, or in other words, any area in which attention is not being paid, is an area left open for the insertion of external messages and control.

Any experience you have without responding to it, or better put, without responding automatically to it, is meditation. Meditation is not necessarily an absence of a response, but it is the insertion of a span of time prior to the response. This pause leads the response to be aware rather than automatic. In fact, in meditation, you practice **not** responding to an experience, in order to break the habit of automatic response. Over one hour you exercise without responding, only experiencing – this is meditation. Afterwards, when you return to action, your responses are no longer automatic, until this soothing of the mind fades away, and a need to restore serenity through meditation arises.

Some people engage in hypnosis and think they are performing meditation. In hypnosis, the activity of thoughts is silenced as well, but hypnosis is not a halt to subconscious activity – on the contrary, it is complete surrender to the subconscious. You seemingly tell the subconscious: "I am stepping aside – you can operate freely." This is the quiet of a person surrendering to pressure, raising his hands. This is not truly quiet, only surrender and willingness to bear the burden and avoid confrontation in return for temporary quiet. So long as man is not fully aware, but also not in a state of total distraction, the subconscious seeks to take over, but encounters the resistance of consciousness. It is out of this conflict between consciousness and subconsciousness that the constant inner chattering derives – a chattering that is derived from the internal deliberations in a person's soul. The moment one party achieves full control, quiet is achieved, for there is no longer any need to make decisions, no hesitation or conflicts – the path forward is clear, and so action flows smoothly, be it conscious or subconscious, depending on who has the upper hand. Meditation grants victory to consciousness, whereas hypnosis, to the subconscious. Meditation is the expansion of the circle of conscious experience to the maximum possible, whereas hypnosis is the reduction of the circle of conscious experience to the minimum possible, by focusing on only one thing, and distracting consciousness away from all other things. Hypnosis is total distraction. Meditation is not necessarily a silencing of thought – rather, it is the silencing of the subconscious activity of thought, which interferes with the activity of conscious thought and generates constant friction. The technique of meditation is to silence for a brief moment all activities of thought, even conscious thought, in order to reveal the subconscious activity in the background, so it can be identified and halted, and then return to conscious activity, free of interference. This is likened to a person in a public forum trying to give a speech, only to be interfered with by the constant catcalls of another person, continuing until the person delivering the speech halts and asks the chairman to silence the heckler, so that he might conclude his speech in peace. When friction ends and thought is silenced, the mind becomes attentive – but attentive to what? In hypnosis, this attentiveness is directed outwards, making a person susceptible to suggestion and external control.

In meditation, thought abates out of awareness, not

distraction, making the mind attentive inwardly to open up to the soft murmur of intuition, which is the voice of the soul arising from within. The soul is a fragment of the divine whole. The soul is an extension of divine consciousness and is always connected to its divine roots. That is why, when a person connects to his soul via meditation, he remains connected and dedicated to the divine. A person's soul is an extension of the divine presence, not separate from it. A person who regularly practices meditation, at least one hour every morning and one hour every evening, becomes far more intuitive, and receives more and better solutions through flashes of sudden insights. What is the practical difference between meditation and hypnosis? A person can listen to the beat of a drum or the playing of the flute, or direct his mind to any other experiential object such as flowing water or burning fire. If he does not focus on the object of observation, only experiences it, in order to maintain his attention on the experience of this moment, so that he will not be distracted towards thoughts, this is meditation. However, if he focuses attention on the object of observation in order to distract his mind from thoughts, he is practicing hypnosis, not meditation. It seems that the difference between meditation and hypnosis is very fine.

In meditation, we do not reprogram the subconscious to suit us. Rather, we deprogram ourselves altogether; we free ourselves from the habits seared into our subconscious to dictate our actions when we are distracted. It is these habits which enable external factors to control our behavior, and it does not matter if these habits were seared into us as a result of the culture in which we grew up in, or from the propaganda to which we were exposed, or the experiences of pleasure and trauma that left their imprint on us. Meditation is letting events occur on their own – without trying to control them, but also without permitting the events to control you. Whether they are external events or internal events. In fact, if you do not try to control events, the events will have no control over you, and no power to irritate you or drive you to distraction.

The drum has always been a central tool for shamans from cultures all over the world. In the Antebellum South of the United States, slaves were forbidden to play the drum, for by listening to the beating of the drum, African shamans could reach a state of trance, where they performed sorcery. Native American shamans and spiritual masters from India also made much use of this drum beating technique. I have read that Sami shamans in Northern Europe could also reach a trancelike state by focusing on the sound of the drum.

Rabbi Abraham, son of the Rambam (**Maimonides**), wrote in his book "The Guide to Serving God" that the Hebrew ancestors were shepherds, so that they might seek solitude and draw away from noise and bustle of villages and cities, and thereby silence their thoughts. It is not for nothing that Rabbi Nachman of Breslau spoke at length concerning shepherds playing the flute. The shepherds would seclude themselves in a remote location and play the flute. This music making, when done with the proper intent, would bring the shepherd to a state of unity with his maker. The prophet Elija used music in order to bring upon himself the spirit of prophecy.

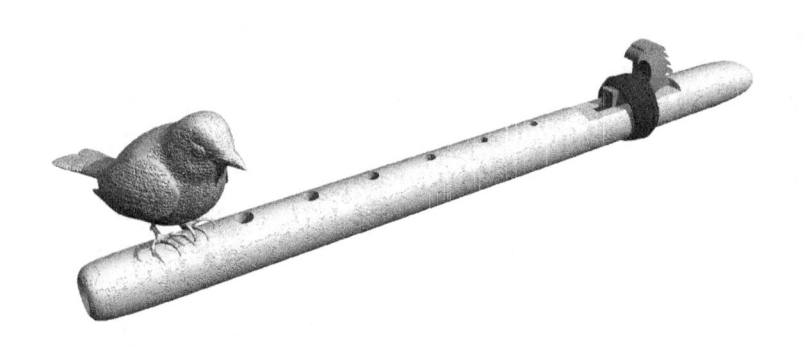

Then it happened, when the musician played, that the hand of the Lord came upon him (Kings 2, 3:16)

Rabbi Nachman of Breslau said the following concerning the importance of music for worship: "Know, that each and every shepherd has a special melody according to the grass and the location where he leads his herd to graze, for each and every animal has a special grass it must eat. Nor does he always graze his herd in the same place. Thus, his melody is dictated according to the grasses and the location where he grazes, for each and every grass has a unique song ... and through the shepherd's knowledge of the right melody to play, by that he gives power to the grasses, and his herd can feed, as it is said, 'The flowers appeared on the earth, the time for song has arrived.' (Song of Songs 2:12) That is, the flowers grow thanks to the song that is theirs... music and song is also good for the shepherd himself, for since the shepherd is always among the animals, it was possible for them to drag his spirit down to bestiality, until the shepherd himself grazes... but through music he is saved from this fate, for music is the refinement of the spirit, sifting the human spirit from the animal, as it is said: 'How can anyone be sure that the spirit of man ascends, while the spirit of the beast descends?' (Ecclesiastes 3:21). For this is the essence of music – to sort the good spirit, as clarified elsewhere." ("Likutey Moharan" – Collected Sayings of Our Teacher, Rabbi Nachman, page 63).

Post-Exercise 4 Report

Take advantage of this moment, just after the exercise while the experience is completely fresh, to fill in the post-exercise report.

Report for exercise 4	Date and time:
Possible influence	Mark with checkmark
I felt calm	
The pace of my thoughts slowed down	
There were moments in which I had no thoughts at all	
I felt emotional discomfort	
I felt physical discomfort	
I felt stress relief	
I experienced involuntary movements	
Old memories were stirred	
I felt like smiling	
I felt inner peace	
At the end, I felt refreshed	

META-COGNITION

There is No confusion in heaven

"There is no joy as great as the resolution of doubt," as the Jewish sages said. Doubt leaves man in a state of uncertainty, in confusion and stress, and this state results in sadness. When doubts are resolved, stress and sadness are gone, and joy results instead.

Meta-cognition is in fact the wisdom of resolving doubts. However we resolve doubt, be it through presumption or through evidence, confusion is eliminated, for we now know what must be done.

Is doubt something that exists in reality, or does it only exist in a person's mind? Is there genuine blurriness in reality, or only in the eye and mind of the beholder?

According to studies in physics performed during the twentieth century, the impression is generated that reality itself contains inherent uncertainty. That is the implication of Heisenberg's uncertainty principle, a fundamental principle of quantum mechanics. You should recall that quantum mechanics is based on scientific experiments. But the truth is that every scientific experiment is performed using tools, and these tools cannot be completely accurate, so by necessity the results they provide cannot be completely clear. Therefore, though this blurring is the result of scientific experiments, it does not indicate a blurriness of reality itself, but of the limited precision of the measuring tools used in the experiment.

The Talmud states that there is no confusion in heaven, that is, any confusion and blurriness from which doubts derive exist only in a person's mind, but there is no absence of knowledge in the heavens, meaning in reality itself there is no uncertainty.

What is this similar to? A person who eagerly drains a cup of yogurt, splashing drops of yogurt on his glasses in the excitement. Now he regularly sees two drops of red yogurt on his glasses, and he fears these are the fiery eyes of a demon who are constantly tracking him, leading him to develop anxieties and fears. But the truth is that he has simply projected the problem with his eyeglasses onto reality.

The same applies to our senses. Our senses have limitations – a limitation of time and a limitation of space. There is a limit to the exposure time of the eye, just as for the camera, and hence a body moving rapidly seems blurred in photos due to the motion-blur. The eye is also limited in the resolution it is capable of perceiving, like a camera, and hence very small or distant objects seem blurred in photos. Does this mean that due to the limitations of the naked eye we will conclude that reality itself is blurred? A drunk or cross-eyed individual who sees everything double might think that everything really was duplicated in reality – two suns rising in the sky every morning, two moons illuminating the night – projecting his eye trouble onto reality. We use sensors and measurement devices whose accuracy is inevitably limited.

There is no reason to decide that this imprecision is an innate quality of reality itself. That is what chaos theory actually says. According to chaos theory, uncertainty derives from the limited precision of our instruments and sensors that we use for measurements, and it is not an innate quality of reality. In reality, there are systems that are extremely complex and complicated, and their behavior is extraordinarily diverse, so to us, they may seem to be acting randomly, when in fact they are operating according to wholly deterministic laws, except we can never predict the behavior of these systems based on their initial conditions. Those initial conditions can never be measured with precision, due to the limits in accuracy of the measurement device, and any little change in the initial conditions of these systems results in a massive change in the final outcome – known as the butterfly effect. An example of such a supposedly chaotic system is the weather.

According to chaos theory, the evidence that a system is not truly random is that order becomes apparent when you collect and examine the data accumulated from monitoring the system and discover that there is order in the data, and that this order has a tendency to arrange itself in fractals. If the system was truly random, it should have generated uniform chaos, homogenously spread out across all places and times, like the white noise or the static snow that fills the television screen when there is no reception.

It seems to us that a system that is hard to predict is random, but that is not the case. Order, even if it is not understood and filled with contradictions, is still order, and order cannot be random. Order can be generated only when there are rules, even if we do not know what those rules are.

To illustrate: if we enter a house and find a massive mess, the requisite conclusion would be that the house was abandoned. But if we enter a house characterized by order, but the order is illogical – the table and chairs are glued to the ceiling; the clothes are folded meticulously in piles stuffed into the refrigerator and so on – it would be clear to us that the house is not abandoned because someone organized it. We would know it had an owner who deliberately organized it in this manner, however illogical it is to us. An abandoned home with no one to maintain it, naturally aspires to disorder, and would become a dump over the years – the roof would begin to leak in a year or two; the furniture would become covered in dust; a careless kick of a ball, by children playing near the house, shatters one of the windows; dogs and cats would soon enter the house through the shattered window and begin to knock things over; an unmaintained house would therefore become a ruin over a few years – this is the principle of entropy ruling over all matter. If we leave a house we own, for many years, and when we return we will find it orderly and clean, then clearly an unwanted guest has taken up habitation within it, no matter how crazy the order is.

MEDITATION — GUIDANCE

Exercise 5

Instructions

It is time for the morning exercise of the third day.

- Look for a quiet place, with a chair you can sit on comfortably.
- Sit straight up, comfortably, preferably without leaning backwards.
- The head should be straight up and comfortable.
- Be sure to keep a clock somewhere nearby.
- The length of the exercise is 20 minutes.
- Start with a few minutes of sitting without doing anything.
- Then begin feeling your breathing.
- After a while, begin repeating the word in your inner speech with every breath.

• • •

A person should set a specific time in the day to halt all activity of the body and simply observe, without thinking and without moving – then he will hear gentle music playing from his soul. These are not waves of sound he hears from his inner soul, but rather waves of inner joy and astonishment at the beauty and magic of existence. Try it yourself. It is hard to silence the body and thought, but if you succeed in this, you are in for a surprise. Perhaps not immediately at first, but if you do so regularly, and get used to devoting a certain amount of time every day to thought free observation, you will undergo a great transformation.

The body does, and the mind thinks, and the soul observes. The soul is the experiencer within man. It is the one thing that feels pleasure or sorrow within man.

When a man is preoccupied with doing, his attention is naturally directed at the body. All the more so if man is occupied in fulfilling his desires, for then his heart is not free for either thought or observation. In order to direct awareness inwards – to the soul, you must first of all halt all activity of the body, ideally at a set time every day, which should be defined as your "quiet hour." You can start with fifteen minutes – in a hyper-active generation such as ours, even fifteen minutes is a good start.

When the activity of the body halts, amplified activity of the thought begins. The silenced body stops providing interest, and one's attention has nothing to grab onto, and hence it turns elsewhere in its search of distraction. The next target of your attention is the mind. That is why inactivity of the body always results in increased activity of the brain. Always when the body is quiet, the mind begins to work overtime. I have run into people who have undergone a great change merely by being forced to sit in an isolated location without anything to do. This forced them to think about things they had never considered before. When the body goes on strike, consciousness moves inwards towards to the mind, and many thoughts begin to surface. These thought also need to be silenced. It is the voice of the soul we wish to hear, not the mind. Thought is also a background noise interfering with our ability to hear the soul.

A prisoner condemned to hard labor, digging endless ditches in the field, cannot stop to admire the scenery around him, he is preoccupied in his work. His consciousness is narrowed and focused on the activity of the body. A businessman, a scientist and a meditator are on the train together. All three look out of the train window at the breathtaking view passing them by. What will the businessman be interested in? The businessman will try to assess the value of the wood logs that can be harvested from the forest outside the window. The scientist will attempt to classify the animals and plants. The meditator? He will simply admire the beauty. Why is this? Because the consciousness of the businessman is identified with his body, while the consciousness of the scientist goes deeper, and is identified with his mind. But the consciousness of the meditator, however, is deeper still and is identified with his soul. The body does, the mind thinks, and the soul observes and admires. If we wish to direct our consciousness deep into the soul, we must first turn off our bodily activity, including movement and as much sensory stimulation as we can. Sit in a comfortable position in a quiet place and close your eyes. After a short time, thoughts begin to surface – because when the body is silent, one begins to think.

Here begins the hard part. The most difficult thing to

do in the process of observation is to silence thoughts. This is much more difficult than silencing the body, for we are used to thinking, but there is also a deeper reason. Giving up thinking is in fact letting go of your ego, which is very difficult. The pleasures of the senses are the lusts of the body, but qualities such as the pursuit of honor, pride and anger are rooted in the mind and the ego generated by thought. Hence, if we want to turn off thought, which means canceling your ego, we should bear in mind that it is not easy, but also not impossible. If you practice this over time, one can gain considerable skill in thought cancelation.

The ability to silence thought has many side benefits. Let us suppose a person must cross a dangerous and narrow bridge a week from now. All week he is anxious and concerned and has no rest. There is no need and no benefit from these concerns and anxieties. Not only do they not help finding solutions for the problems the person must deal with, but they also sully his mood and drain his strength. This person, who must cross a dangerous and narrow bridge a week from now, spends all day worrying about it and is restless. He spent an entire week troubled, unable to enjoy all his plentitude and unable to see it or be thankful to it, and when finally the time comes to actually cross the bridge, he is already exhausted and lacks the mental reserves to see it through. Therefore, the ability to turn off troublesome thoughts has great advantages in the efficient conduct of action as well. That is how a person learns how to live in the moment, and his anxieties are short-lived, focusing solely on the time of trial. At all other times, he is relaxed, gathering his strength for the trial to come. The life of a man who cannot stop worrying is no life at all. This is particularly true for the faithful man, for whom it is right to trust in the Creator of the World, and hence he had best learn to silence his thoughts, and not to worry too much about tomorrow. But even without faith in a higher power, quality of life is reason enough to learn how to turn off troubling thoughts.

Let us take for example a man who decides to kill himself even though he is completely healthy. Say he has lost his fortune in the stock market, and is left destitute, and hence he decides to leap off the roof. But this man lacks nothing, every organ in his body is sound – why then should he wish to kill himself? Go out to the garden, buy something to eat, enjoy a few more beautiful moments of life – the shining sun, the blue sky and the chirping birds. Why in the world kill yourself? What is dampening his mood? – thoughts! He is thinking about what he had, what he has lost, and that is leading him to despair. Had he known to soothe his thoughts, his life would be back on track.

I once read a story about a woman who despised her husband. She blamed him for sending her only son to drive her father and mother-in-law to the airport. On the road, they suffered an accident, and her only son died in it. Matters deteriorated so badly that she filed for divorce, and her hate consumed her so much that she even hired an assassin to murder her husband. But then she went out to the street and was assaulted by muggers. She suffered a serious blow to the head, and her entire memory was wiped clean. Now she must relearn everything, yet free of the evil memory of the past. In the hospital, she is told her name, and her husband comes to visit her. Suddenly her husband seems to her to be a very nice man, and she is content in what she has. The husband on his part keeps mum. He does not tell her they were in the middle of divorce proceedings, because this is a chance to start again. What then was the problem? Nothing, all that was needed was to erase the hard disk and all was well. It is thoughts of the past that generated the entire problem.

When a man learns to soothe his thoughts, he ceases being bitter. His anger at the injustice of the world (and it only seems unjust due to the limits of his understanding) goes away – he learns to observe the world without judging what he sees. Had we seen the world clearly, free of thoughts and criticism, we would have effortlessly arrived, awed at the beauty and magic of existence. Thoughts are the greatest obstacle on the road to awe.

Now that we have set a "quiet hour" for ourselves each day, it is time to ask – what is the technique? How does one truly soothe one's thoughts? The technique is simple – anchor your attention in the experience of this moment. In the book Derech HaMelech (*The Way of the King*), written by Rabbi Kalonymus Kalman Shapira, another idea is presented: observe the thoughts themselves. The moment you observe these thoughts, you are no longer thinking them, merely experiencing them, and they fade away on their own. But it is not enough to return your attention to the experiential plane, every time you notice attention escaping to your thoughts. You also need to keep it in place, on the experience, for as much time as possible, effortlessly, but consistently and with full wakeful awareness of how thoughts lay in ambush to steal away our attention constantly. It is not merely that foreign thoughts seek to steal away our attention while we are practicing the "soothing" of our thoughts. Rather, that is a mechanism intended to block the path to anyone not yet worthy from ascending to the rarified heights of spirituality. The Baal-Shem-Tov, founder of Hasidic Judaism, said that a man who is dedicated in his prayer, rises up until he is about to enter a high spiritual plane. If he is unworthy to enter this plane, he is tossed a foreign thought to distract his attention, confusing his prayer and ejecting him outwards. However, said the Baal-Shem-Tov, one must nonetheless continue pushing himself onwards, knocking on heaven's door and not give up. That is how one makes progress.

When thoughts are silent, that is a sign that your consciousness is now rooted at your soul, and your soul is now in control. You can now halt your observation – there is no more need of it – and wait for the awe that pours in on its own. Awe leads you to feel joy and loving identification with all of creation.

At the conclusion of the "quiet hour," when you return to deal with your everyday business, you are no longer the same person. Everything appears to you differently. More beautiful, finer. And even if you are angry at something, that anger is not deep, and you easily forgive and forget. You learn to place greater weight on observation than thought, and this settles you. Your need to satisfy the lusts of the body also decreases for an inner light of joy shines from within, freeing you from dependence on sensual pleasures. That does not mean you will no longer encounter difficulties and challenges – only that these difficulties will not spoil your "inner celebration."

In his book "Faith and Trust," Rabi Avrohom Yeshaya Karelitz wrote as follows:

"The virtue of faith is a fine sensibility of the soul. If man is soulful, and is at peace within himself, free of sensual hunger, then his eye burns bright with the scenery of high skies and deep earth, and he is thrilled and in awe, for the world seems to him like an inexplicable riddle, wondrous and mysterious, and this riddle enfolds his heart and mind, and he nearly faints, bereft of the breath of life, and he is fully dedicated to this riddle, and the thought of solving it consumes his soul, and he is prepared to walk through fire and water for it, for what is life to him, if this pleasant life obscures from him the hidden purpose, and his soul is dizzy and mournful and yearning to understand its secret and know its root, and the gates are locked."

Post-Exercise 5 Report

Take advantage of this moment, when you are right after the exercise, and the experience is completely fresh, to fill in the post-exercise report.

Report for exercise 5	Date and time:
Possible influence	Mark with checkmark
I felt calm	
The pace of my thoughts slowed down	
There were moments in which I had no thoughts at all	
I felt emotional discomfort	
I felt physical discomfort	
I felt stress relief	
I experienced involuntary movements	
Old memories were stirred	
I felt like smiling	
I felt inner peace	
At the end, I felt refreshed	

META-COGNITION

Knowledge and internalization

In previous chapters, we spoke much about meta-cognition, which is the study of thought processes.

But correct thinking, without internalization, generates no change in practice.

Correct thinking can lead to the knowledge of truth – good and well – but knowing the truth, in and of itself, without any internalization, is pointless. In other words, if even after the truth comes out one continues to hesitate instead of standing up, taking action, and implementing that which has become known in full and certain clarity, such knowledge has no practical benefit.

In this too, meditation comes to our aid. As part of releasing that which is imprisoned and repressed in the subconscious, meditation enables repressed knowledge to rise to the threshold of consciousness, so that it is internalized, accepted by the heart, and practically influence our lives. Eventually, awareness is a way of bringing the heart to emotionally accept what the mind knows, so that a connection is formed between the mind and the heart. This is the essence of awareness, the ability to accept information emotionally, because from the beginning, repression is derived from an unwillingness or inability to accept information emotionally. On the level of the mind, the knowledge exists and is recorded, but the subconscious obscures it, for we lack the emotional will or fortitude to accept it. That is why we turn our mind to distraction, taking this unwanted information out of the circle of attention, by focusing on other things.

This basically means that meditation begins with awareness and ends in awareness; it starts with awareness of thoughts and ends with awareness of emotions.

That is why the meditator is a person who is in awe of what he experiences, just like a child. The experiences pierce the open heart of the meditator, and results in an upswell of emotions, whether awe, excitement, or horror – like a child whose heart is still pure, unsullied by repressions and traumas that usually accumulate down the road. The meditator does not need a sharp pain to penetrate the barrier between heart and mind in order to be shocked into performing a change in his life. He lacks the iron barrier separating the mind from the heart, a barrier that those who do not practice meditation all too often develop.

MEDITATION — GUIDANCE

Exercise 6

Instructions

It is time for the evening exercise of the third day.
- Look for a quiet place, with a chair you can sit on comfortably.
- Sit straight up, comfortably, preferably without leaning backwards.
- The head should be straight up and comfortable.
- Be sure to keep a clock in sight.
- The length of the exercise is 20 minutes.
- Start with a few minutes of sitting without doing anything.
- Then begin feeling your breathing.
- After a while begin repeating the word in your inner speech with every breath.

● ● ●

The nervous system creates the connection between the body and the soul. The soul yearns for the feeling of pleasure provided to it by the nervous system, through the body, and hence it is clingy and yearns for the body. The problem is that this same nervous system that transmits to the soul the sensations of pleasure, also transmits the sensations of pain. Thus, when the soul turns its attention to the sensation, in pursuit of pleasure, it inadvertently also exposes itself to sensations of pain. The sensation of pleasure is the bait that draws people to focus on sensations, and then they are smacked with the punishment of being seduced to pleasure, and that punishment is pain – truly, there is no good without bad.

In meditation you learn to observe sensations and thereby learn to recognize the fact that they are not part of you, for if they were a part of you, how could you observe them? The observer needs to stand outside the object of observation. The understanding that arises from observing sensations, that they are a thing apart from you, leads the soul to stop identifying with the body and its sensations. Thus, a person frees himself from the bonds of the body, and from the control it has over the soul, and becomes truly free. A free person is not a person who has the means to realize his desires – such a person is bound by desire. A truly free person is freed of desire itself.

• • •

A man came to a famous meditation teacher with a question.

"Master," he asked, "why do we suffer?"

The teacher responded: "Because we desire."

The man was surprised: "But is it not natural to desire? How can one not desire?"

The teacher smiled and said: "Desire is like fire. It can provide heat and light, but it can also burn and destroy. You must learn to control your desires, and use them wisely, rather than let them control you."

The man considered this and said: "But how can I control my desires?"

The teacher responded: "Through meditation, you can develop awareness and insight about your thoughts and feelings. By observing them without judgment or attachment, you will be able to free yourself from their grip."

The man was inspired by the words of the teacher and became his student. He devoted himself to the practice of meditation. Over time, he discovered that his desires no longer reigned over him, and that he was capable of living a peaceful life of contentment.

• • •

Not every action generates a distraction and impairs awareness. It is specifically, a goal focused action that serves as a distraction whereas spontaneous action does not distract. The focus on a goal is the essence of desire. A man who does not desire, who is not preoccupied with what the future holds, flows with reality wherever it should lead him. A religious person who truly trusts in providence, finds it easier to forsake his desire to control reality. He has a certain advantage in this, given that faith requires he put his trust in God, and that gives him the mental base for a worry-free life.

Post-Exercise 6 Report

Take advantage of this moment, when you are right after the exercise, and the experience is completely fresh, to fill in the post-exercise report.

Report for exercise 6	Date and time:
Possible influence	Mark with checkmark
I felt calm	
The pace of my thoughts slowed down	
There were moments in which I had no thoughts at all	
I felt emotional discomfort	
I felt physical discomfort	
I felt stress relief	
I experienced involuntary movements	
Old memories were stirred	
I felt like smiling	
I felt inner peace	
At the end, I felt refreshed	

SUMMARY

Meditation is the drug of life

Consciousness transforming chemical substances

There is a group of chemicals known as "empathogens." These substances trigger a state of empathy – as someone who tried them described: "They make you love everyone." The term "empathogen," which means "generating a state of empathy," was coined in the years 1983-1984 by Ralph Metzner. The most renowned of these chemicals is MDMA.

Alexander "Sasha" Theodore Shulgin, June 17, 1925 – June 2, 2014, was a curative chemist, biochemist, organic chemist, pharmacologist, psychopharmacologist and American writer. He was the one who introduced the use of MDMA to psychological care in the late 1970s.

In 1966, Shulgin quit his job to devote himself entirely to the study of psychoactive drugs – drugs that alter the mind. In the mid-1960s, he reinstated an obscure drug that had been patented but then ignored, it was called: methylenedioxymethamphetamine – 3,4, MDMA for short, which would later acquire a street name: "Ecstasy." If there is one place on earth where it all began, it is in California, in a small home laboratory of a man known as the Godfather of Ecstasy.

This chemical did not exist in nature until a worker in the German Pharmaceutical company Merck accidentally synthesized it in the company labs in 1912. Since the new molecule was not found to possess a useful purpose, MDMA remained a formula on fading paper for over 60 years. Upon Germany's defeat in WWI, MDMA, along with all other patent protected pharmaceuticals developed in Germany, were transferred to the labs of the Western Allies as war booty. Its existence faded away from memory, until the Cold War forced the Pentagon to reconsider the potential of this chemical for war. Since it was found to be useless for that as well, it remained on the shelf, gathering dust.

Dr. Shulgin was familiar with this forgotten chemical and thought to himself: "If it was never orally ingested, I wonder what will happen if we try. Let's try this at a 50-milligram dosage." And once again he tried the medication orally at a 100 mg dosage. Then he noticed something was happening.

Dr. Shulgin carried out the first recorded experiment concerning the impact of ecstasy and published a paper about the results of his research, in which he described the impact of the substance. Some of his psychiatrist friends were exposed to the study data and decided to try the drug out, first on themselves, and then on their patients. In the psychotherapeutic community, MDMA is called "empathy." Its impact is equivalent to an entire year of emotional therapy within the space of 6 hours. As soon as psychotherapists began using it, with good results, this drug became quite popular, but not as Dr. Shulgin had hoped, for it became a drug taken at raves. "It turned into a party escape-drug," said Dr. Shulgin, "and I'm sorry to say I'm not happy with that..."

"We have receptors for psychedelic drugs, in our brain, but we don't have psychedelic drugs inside of us. Why do we have the receptors and not the drugs?" asked Dr. Shulgin. "Well, perhaps at one time we had the drugs in our body – as part of a metabolic process we generated the drugs that made the psychedelic state a natural state, and the people living back then, I can see the potential of them looking at the tooth of a tiger and saying: oh look at the pretty design of this tooth, and as a consequence of dropping their defenses against an enemy, they would be removed from the gene-pool, so perhaps those people who did get turned-on because of indigenous-psychedelics (produced in their body) were removed from the gene-pool, and therefore they are no longer here; the drugs are no longer made in the body, but the receptors are still there, because the receptors were not the hazard, it was the drug that was generated in the body that was the hazard to survival, and maybe that is why some of these plants with their psychedelic components, turn you on, because the receptors are intact from previous generations, but the natural psychedelic metabolite in the body no longer exists," said Dr. Shulgin in an interview for a documentary film.

Dr. Shulgin, explains the effect of these drugs: "Part of self-preservation, is to ignore 99% of the stuff that is out there. If you have a person that is observing everything, and remembers everything, he can't cross the street, because he is fascinated by the green lights, by the cars, by the gravel, by the flies that are over there, by the fact that a car has a little flickering turn light, and if he pays attention to everything he sees, it would be a life-risk to cross the street, so he learned to turn that off. He has to watch for the light to turn green! Watch for the first step he makes, watch where his foot goes, glance right and left to see that no cars are coming, and that is how you get across the street safely: you have to ignore 99% of what is around you, in order to be safe, to achieve what you want to achieve. What these things (like ecstasy) catalyze is, they are letting you access these things that you have been ignoring or had been denying."

Dr. Shulgin examined the impact of Ecstasy and other Empathogens on himself for years, and his conclusion was, according to the citation above, that these substances scatter the focus of your attention. You need this focus in order to implement things in the demanding environment where we live, but the result of focusing on achieving goals is the loss of the ability to look in wonder at the beauty surrounding you, as a child does, because you need to stay focused on what is vital for your mission.

Action requires focus, and focus leads to distraction, and thereby causes you to lose your awareness. Focus leads to distraction, because if you are focused on one thing, you become distracted from everything else – you become unaware of everything else. Awareness can only be achieved by turning your attention to the experience. Action slays awareness. Action shrinks your bubble of attention and attentiveness into a tiny dot, while directing your attention to the experiential plain enables that bubble to expand, and this is an aware state of mind. What is awareness? It is an expansion of the bubble of attentiveness and attention. The more you become aware, the more you become empathic.

The reason we have in our mind receptors for substances that alter our consciousness into a state of awareness and empathy is because even today, just as in the distant past, the body **can** be induced to manufacture these substances, without depending on an external supply from drugs such as ecstasy. It is meditation that leads us to enter this state of mind, leading the body to release these substances, without taking artificial substances that always have negative side effects. Meditation is the drug of life, a drug that does not result in any damage. Just as during times of stress and anxiety the body secretes a certain type of chemical substances, when the energy in our nervous system is peaceful and serene, the body secretes other substances, for body and mind are bound to one another.

The substances secreted by the body in stressful situations are not healthy to the body, but they are required for its survival. The substances secreted by the body during calmness and tension release, a state one reaches via meditation, are substances that are healthy for the body and the soul. That is why we have these receptors in our brain – survival does not require us to be in a constant state of stress. On the contrary, once the fight or flight situation is over, the body and soul need to recuperate by releasing the stress accumulated during the conflict, so that the system can heal. That is precisely what we do in meditation.

TO CONCLUDE

In conclusion

Now that the series of six exercises over three days is concluded, I hope you have internalized the principle. You need to carry on in the same way going forward, and it is best you continue filling in the reports after each exercise, or after every few exercises. Print out additional reports and fill them out at least once a week for some time. Look at the questionnaire you filled out at the beginning and compare your stress levels every month, for a period of time. See if your stress level decreases over time. Why fill out the reports? Since the impact of meditation is very gradual, at least for some people, and it is a little hard to notice if you do not pay attention to it. Besides, people have a tendency to forget bad things that took place in the past, while taking the present good for granted. By filling out the reports, we help ourselves devote attention to changes taking place in the stress level from which we suffer, and how this stress level declines the more you persist in practicing meditation. Most of those who ceased practicing meditation, did so because they didn't notice the change taking place in them. So continue both practicing and recording the effect this exercise has on you, through reports, and then you will learn to appreciate what you receive from the meditation, and this will spur you to continue practicing.

That's it, I have finished what I had to say. I have collected the information I presented in this manual from many different sources, learning all that I could from anyone offering a fresh insight. My initial exposure to meditation was from Jewish sources, after encountering it explicitly in the article of silence as it appears in the book "Derech HaMelech" (*The Way of the King*), written by Kalonymus Kalman Shapira. Once I realized that this was indeed Jewish-style meditation, though it was called by a different name, so I began dealing with it, as well as cross-referencing information from Jewish sources with other sources. I wandered through meditation forums on the internet and learned a great deal. I listened to lectures provided by important meditation teachers from India, as they are doubtless authoritative sources on meditation techniques. I learned quite a bit from psychology textbooks. Of course, I did not take any personal views, or the ritual-religious aspects of the Indian traditions, only the technical-practical knowledge that aided me with the exercise itself. After collecting all the knowledge, I derived my own conclusions from it, and provided explanations that seemed to me correct. In my opinion, whoever wishes to enter the field of meditation, will find much useful knowledge in this manual.

Best of luck to you.

Yishai Shiloh

APPENDIX A

The essence of matter

Concerning the question of whether there is absolute truth, we are left with one issue to clarify: in science two opposites have been proven to apply to a single phenomenon. Various scientific studies have shown light to be both a particle and a wave, even though these are opposite manifestations of a single phenomenon. We have already stated that generally speaking, the scientific method of investigation is good, so how is it possible that in science as well, we encounter a situation in which two opposites have been proven to be factually true?

The physicists have studied light and asked themselves – what is light? Is it a wave, like sound waves? And like sound waves are motion that passes through matter, but is not matter, so too do light waves pass through matter, and the reason light passes through space as well, obligates us to say that space is filled with some form of matter called "ether" that suffuses the entire universe. Or is light a stream of particles of matter? As usual in science, one does not argue too much, but lets reality speak, which means conducting experiments to confirm one hypothesis and refute the other. However, the experiments being conducted proved both hypotheses – that is light is both a particle and a wave, even though they are mutually exclusive. A particle is a body, whereas a wave is bodiless motion; a particle occupies a point in space, whereas a wave is spread over space. So how can both mutually exclusive models coexist?! And how is it possible that experiments alternately show light to display properties only a particle possesses, whereas on other occasions light reveals properties characteristic only of a wave?

If you thought that this contradiction that was revealed in the study of light is unique to light alone, and is an unusual property, then you are mistaken. It has turned out to be true in regard to all subatomic particles. The question therefore applies not only to light, but to matter in general – what is matter?

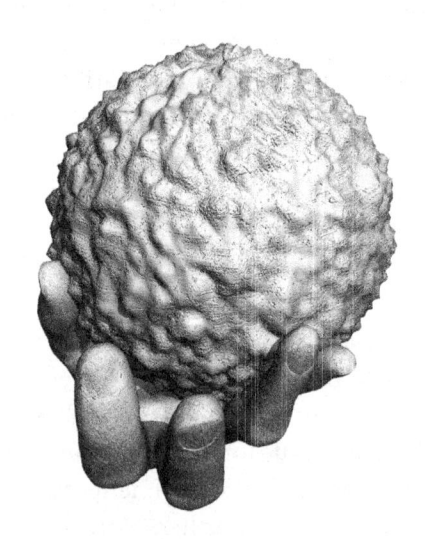

What is the matter that fills up the form?

Let's be clear, starting at the beginning. Let us observe for a moment the composition of matter. Is matter composed of particles? At first glance, this appears to be the case, but it is not so! Matter is made up of motion, not particles, and I am saying nothing new by stating this. As it is well established, the amount of particles filling the volume of the material is negligible. The material is composed of atoms, which are very small particles. Atoms in turn are composed of a nucleus, which contains protons and neutrons, and an outer envelope made up of electrons that rapidly revolve around the nucleus. The illusion of volume of the matter is generated by the rapid movement of electrons around the nucleus. If you halt the electrons in their track, all of the matter in the world will fade away into nothing. If the gaps between the particles of which the atom is composed are eliminated, then a body the size of a football field will shrink to the size of a cherry pit. It follows that the volume of matter is filled by motion rather than particles. Particles make up a minute fraction of the total volume of matter.

If it were possible to freeze time, halting any movement, and the world would freeze, then matter would not exist. Matter as we know it does not truly exist in external reality, it exists only in the meeting place between senses and reality, and even this only in relation to the individual who experiences it, not in reality itself.

Let us take for example the sense of sight. It can be likened to a camera. Every camera has its limitations. The first limitation: a limited length of exposure. This means the camera absorbs the image of reality at a given moment, let us say a thousandth of a second. What happens if an object moves before a camera very rapidly, so that in a thousandth of a second it succeeds in moving a significant distance, from point A to point B? How would this object look in a photo taken with this camera? It would look as if it were both at point A and point B and a sort of a smeared superposition would be generated between points A and B. That is what we see in photos of a rapidly moving object – a streak is formed, and the image of the rapidly moving body is smeared. If the exposure time of the camera were shorter, denying the object the possibility of moving significantly during the exposure, this smearing would not be present.

The camera has a second limitation, a limitation of its separation level (resolution). That is, a camera cannot take a picture of a body smaller than the "pixel" of that camera. If we photograph two bodies that are smaller than the separation level of the camera, and both enter under the same "pixel" in the photograph, the photograph will show as if the two bodies are merged into one, positioned in the same spot. This is an illusion, but it is this illusion that generates the reality of matter. Matter is a result of these limitations of resolution and exposure time. The reason matter seems continuous and full is that electrons are very small, and move so rapidly, that it seems to us as if they are superimposed over all possible locations around the nucleus, but this is not truly the case. Insofar as our senses are concerned, this is indeed the way things are, for each of these senses suffers the limitation of exposure time and resolution, just as the camera does. Even our sense of touch is bound by these limitations, so we can feel matter, and in terms of the senses it constitutes a tangible reality for all intents and purposes. But insofar as existence in reality beyond sensory perceptions, there is nothing beyond movement here.

The famous scientist Albert Einstein demonstrated that matter can be transformed into energy, which was the theoretical basis of the creation of the atom bomb. In truth, matter is energy rather than matter – as explained above, it is composed of motion rather than particles. The atom bomb splits the structure of the atom, in which small particles rapidly rotate around the nucleus; the particles split from the structure of the atom are flung out all over the place, at rapid speed and enormous numbers, colliding into the surrounding atoms and destabilizing them. That is how the massive heat wave released by the nuclear explosion is formed – this heat is the motion of matter's particles. Thermal energy is the kinetic energy of vibrating and colliding atoms in a substance.

The radiation released from a radioactive material also derives from particles released from the structure of the atom. Radioactive material is material whose atomic structure is unstable, and hence it naturally breaks down over time. That is, particles break out of its structure, scattering all over the place, and that is what we call "radiation." Uranium is used to manufacture an atom bomb. It is an unstable material, and it is enriched into an even more unstable form. The first bomb had a relatively simple structure – two lumps of uranium wrapped with explosives. When the explosives were ignited, the two uranium lumps were hurled into one another, leading to a chain reaction in which each Uranium atom, as it split, hurled its subatomic particles, which then collided with the nuclei of adjacent uranium atoms, leading them to split as well in a chain reaction that released massive amounts of energy. What energy? The motion energy that had been stored beforehand in the nucleus, in the closed structure, where particles rapidly rotated around the nucleus and were then flung out of this structure with incredible force. The particles released from the pre-split structure realign into new matter-structures, and thus new materials are generated out of the split uranium atom, restoring stability. However, the destruction of the previous atomic structure generates the massive heat wave released in a nuclear explosion. This is a rather oversimplified explanation, but our purpose here is simplification for the sake of illustration of one important point – matter is composed of motion. This is the reason one can transform matter into energy, because when the nucleus splits, particles cease revolving around the nucleus and scatter in all directions, impacting the atoms around them, leading them to vibrate, releasing the heat, which is actually the vibrations of these matter particles. In the case of unstable material, such as enriched uranium, the impact of particles leads atoms to not only vibrate, but also split, resulting in a chain reaction.

Albert Einstein coined the "quantum mechanism" theory originally, or to be more accurate, he was the one who pointed out that light was both a particle and a wave, even though they were supposedly mutually exclusive models. For suggesting this, he won at first an outpouring of scorn, until empirical data from experiments validated his claim. Nonetheless, Einstein found it very hard to accept the implied conclusion from this finding – that reality is not deterministic, which means it is not absolute. Is it possible to state that by observing a given object, man makes it real? Or at least materially real? The renowned Danish scientist Niels Bohr believed so, but Albert Einstein never felt comfortable with this conception. Indeed, Einstein mocked Bohr's claim by saying: "Do you truly believe the moon does not exist unless we look at it?"

There is no need to go so far as to say that observation generates matter from nothing. Matter does not form by observation. In practice, nothing is formed by observation. These are two aspects of the reality of matter. These are two viewpoints that are simultaneously true. One is true in regard to the senses, whereas the other is true in regard to that which lies beyond the senses. The two cannot be reconciled, and nor do they need to be reconciled. The attempt to seek out a theory explaining how the two are compatible is the error.

One might conclude that the result of scientific research concerning the nucleus, showing that two mutually exclusive theorems can be proven, indicates that there is no absolute truth in scientific research. This conclusion is false, because this wave-particle or energy-matter duality is not truly a contradiction, as explained above.

APPENDIX B

The basis of all religions

The basis of all religions is the recognition that consciousness exists even without the body. Those who believe consciousness cannot independently exist without the body, are missing a very important point without which neither religion nor spirituality can be understood.

As for me, I never understood why it should be so difficult to accept the possibility of a bodyless, spiritual entity. After all, computer technology also maintains a distinction between software and hardware. True, this is not quite the same as the division between spirit and matter, for software is data that needs to be saved in hardware, otherwise it will be lost, whereas our claim is that spirit or consciousness is not a product of matter, and its existence does not depend on matter. Nonetheless, for the sake of illustration, the separation between hardware and software can be used. What is important to know is that consciousness and the thoughts it is generating in the mind are not merely electric signals in the mind, it is another layer of reality, which contains an entire world. Consciousness has an objective reality, not merely a subjective one, just as matter does.

This insight, that consciousness can exist independently of matter, and continues long after the body rots away in the earth, leads us to see things differently. It makes us cease judging everything based on economic success. If you know that everything material passes – all beautiful movie actors grow old and their beauty fades away – you seek out spiritual pleasures that are an inseparable part of you and will not leave you even when your body dies.

The only way to achieve a clear awareness that consciousness can exist even without the body, and that there is life after death, is through meditation. Some people are able to achieve an out-of-body-experience through meditation, whereas others, even if they cannot achieve full separation from the body, reach the awareness that the body, and thought as well, are things that stand outside the self. I heard about a meditator who very much loved to perform meditation, and one day he had an out-of-body experience spontaneously, without knowing or expecting that meditation might bring him to this state. This experience was so traumatic for him that he never practiced meditation again.

There is also another way of reaching the awareness that consciousness exists without the body. Indeed, this awareness will come to all of us – on the day we die. However, at this point, it is too late for this awareness to have a chance to influence life. One may also have an out-of-body experience during clinical death, but that is hardly something one wants to aim for or have any control over. We are therefore left with meditation alone.

Spiritual Entities

In order to communicate with spiritual entities, one must ascend to the spirit world. This cannot be accomplished in an ordinary state of consciousness. In this too, meditation assists us, for it releases the bonds of consciousness from the body, and that is the only state in which one can communicate with spiritual entities.

Prophets had techniques meant to trigger a trancelike state leading to prophecy. The prophet was not a passive practitioner of the prophecy he received. There were some techniques the students of the prophet learned from him. In order to receive prophecy one needs to develop a channel of communications with the spirit world. The great question is: Who is picking up the phone on the other side of the line?

And this makes all the difference. When the prophet is granted spiritual ascension, he must be pure so that he may come in contact with pure beings, and not be possessed by evil spirits who will harm him and seek to use his body for nefarious purposes.

In various mystical teachings, there are descriptions of locations and entities one can meet in the spirit world. In Judaism, the design of the habitations of the Tribes of Israel during their sojourn in the desert, as well as the design of the Temple in Jerusalem, are a reflection of what exists in the supernal realm, sort of a road map for the prophet.

According to Jewish kabbalah, the location the prophet should connect to is the Tree of Life. In the center of the Tree of Life is the divine presence, surrounded by the four archangels, who are likened to the legs of its throne.

The archangels are named: Michael, Gabriel, Uriel and Raphael, and they are in charge of both the four cardinal directions and the four elements: air, water, earth and fire. The four archangels each have three subordinate second tier angels, each charged with one of the twelve signs of the zodiac and the forces they represent. Subordinated to each of the dozen second tier angels are half a dozen third tier angels, revolving around the second circle, and each of these seventy-two angels is charged with one of the nations of the world, which their root is also part of the Tree of Life.

The synagogue mosaic in Beit Alpha, showing the zodiac. 5th century AD

The prophets of Israel paid no heed and did not seek out angels that are not included in the tree of Life, for any spiritual entity that is not included in the tree of life, mixes good and evil, truth and falsehood, and cannot be relied upon.

This structure of the Tree of Life is alluded to in the order of the establishment of the camps of the tribes in the desert. The *Mishkan*, the "temporary Temple" of the Jewish people during the Exodus, is called the "*Shechina* camp" (divine presence camp). In the circle surrounding the Shechina camp is the camp titled the "the Levite camp" with four sub encampments: the priestly families, and the tent of Moses, camped in the East. In the three other cardinal directions were the three Levite families – the Merari family in the North, the Gershon family in the West, and the Kehat family in the south. In the third circle, called the "Israel camp" were the twelve tribes, who were divided into four groups of three tribes – Judah, Issachar and Zebulon camped in the East; Dan, Asher and Naphtali camped in the North; Menashe, Ephraim and Binyamin camped in the West; Reuven, Simon and Gad camped in the South. The impure would be excluded from some of the camps, depending on the type of impurity. Some impure people would be excluded from all three camps – the Shechina camp, the Levite camp and the Israel Camp as well. Other impure people would be excluded from the Shechina and Levite camps, but not the Israel camp. And some impurities would only be excluded from the Shechina camp.

When the prophet is granted spiritual ascension, and walks the path of paradise, he must be pure to be permitted entry to the camps of the sacred angels. If he is impure, he is excluded from their presence, just as the impure were excluded from the three camps in the desert. God set the flaming sword toward the path of the tree of life, to prevent impure men from walking the path to the tree of life and feeding on its fruits.

APPENDIX C

Separation of law from justice in religious legal systems

The separation of law from justice exists in religious legal systems, not necessarily in secular religious systems. Religions usually calcify over time, leaving only a shell of practices: rituals, traditions and rites. Their spiritual aspect gradually fades away and is forgotten. In the Jewish religion as well, one can see the phenomena taking roots over time. Some movements sought to correct this problem. The Hassidic movement sought to restore to Judaism its spiritual roots and vibrancy; the "*mussar*" (moral) movement sought to restore to Judaism the values and morality that had been forgotten during life's troubles. These movements failed to fix the problem at its root, because eventually they sought to add spiritual or moral awareness to the practical laws of *halakha*, to prevent them from becoming automatic and pointless actions. But they never sought to **subordinate** the halakhah to spirituality and morality; they did not subject law to justice. The only man who raised such a suggestion was Rabbi Shimon Bar Yohai, who ruled that the practical implementation of the rules of halakha change in accordance with the purpose for which they were set, and his method is known throughout the Talmud as unique.

Clearly, law without morality does not truly change people, but even habituating people to learn morality alongside learning the practical halakhic portion will not fix anything, because if the spirit of the law has no practical impact on how it is implemented, the spiritual-moral aspect of it remains toothless and irrelevant.

Rabbi Shimon Bar Yohai's approach was never adopted as the norm in halakhic interpretation. The norm today is that where the spirit and letter of the law come into conflict – it is the letter of the law that prevails.

The method of Rabbi Shimon Bar Yohai, in contrast, is to seek the reasons for the laws the Bible dictates to us. The question is, what is meant by "reasons" – is this the purpose or the cause for the law?

According to Judaism, God's commandments are the divine will. Divine will has no cause, for no power compels the creator of the world to want something. The divine will is metaphysical, and does not change according to the circumstances, for there is no change in the divine. And that will does not exist for the sake of maintaining the world of matter – the Sabbath is not a social law, and the "*shmita*" year, in which no agricultural work should be done, is not an agricultural lesson – on the contrary, the material world into which we descend when we receive a material body to embody our soul is meant to enable us to maintain a spiritual life within the darkness of materialism.

However, if by "reason" we mean a purpose, rather than a cause, then certainly the commandments of the Bible serve a purpose and the way of implementing them, might vary according to the circumstances. If we are not mindful of the purpose God sought to achieve through his commandments, then we inevitably end up with hollow ritual and calcified religion.

This is likened to the story about the trained bear whose master asked that he watch over him during his afternoon nap, and make sure no one disturb his sleep. Shortly after the master fell into slumber, a fly appeared and began to pester the master, landing on his forehead. What did the clumsy bear do? He picked up a rock, and crushed the fly – and his master's skull...

Made in the USA
Las Vegas, NV
08 April 2025